Spiritual Medicine

Master Energetic Healing and Meditation Through the Practices of Acupressure, Reiki, Crystal Healing, and More

Kara Lawrence

© **Copyright 2020 - All rights reserved.**

The content contained within this book may not be reproduced, duplicated or transmitted without direct written permission from the author or the publisher.

Under no circumstances will any blame or legal responsibility be held against the publisher, or author, for any damages, reparation, or monetary loss due to the information contained within this book, either directly or indirectly.

Legal Notice:

This book is copyright protected. It is only for personal use. You cannot amend, distribute, sell, use, quote or paraphrase any part, or the content within this book, without the consent of the author or publisher.

Disclaimer Notice:

Please note the information contained within this document is for educational and entertainment purposes only. All effort has been executed to present accurate, up to date, reliable, complete information. No warranties of any kind are declared or implied. Readers acknowledge that the author is not engaged in the rendering of legal, financial, medical or professional advice. The content within this book has been derived from various sources. Please consult a licensed professional before attempting any techniques outlined in this book.

By reading this document, the reader agrees that under no circumstances is the author responsible for any losses, direct or indirect, that are incurred as a result of the use of the information contained within this document, including, but not limited to, errors, omissions, or inaccuracies.

Table of Contents

INTRODUCTION 1
   WHAT TO EXPECT 2
      Your Self and Yourself 4
      Further Reading 6

CHAPTER 1: TRUE HEALING 7
   THE LONG HISTORY OF SPIRITUAL HEALING 10
   HEALING HOLISTICALLY 14
      More Than Medicine 16
      Repetition and Reinforcement 18

CHAPTER 2: SPIRITUAL ENERGY AND YOU 21
   THE MANY SPIRITS 24
      The Soulful Spirit 26
      The Energetic Spirit 27
      The Emotional Spirit 30
   ENERGY AND BALANCE 32
      Negative and Positive Energy 36
      Alignment 38
      Synchrony is Healing 41

CHAPTER 3: CHANNELING THROUGH THE BODY 43
   BODYWORK METHODS 45
      Acupressure and Reflexology 47
      Yoga 53
      Breathwork 58
      New Experiences Nourish the Body 63

CHAPTER 4: CHANNELING THROUGH THE MIND 67
   THE MIND AS A TOOL 69
      Visualization and Affirmation 72

Aromatherapy *82*
Nurturing the Mind with Acceptance *88*

CHAPTER 5: CHANNELING THROUGH THE SPIRIT 91

REVISITING THE SPIRIT.. 94
Reiki *96*
Crystal Healing *104*
Know Your Spirit *109*

CHAPTER 6: MEDITATION 111

PREPARING YOURSELF FOR MEDITATION 112
SYNCHRONIZING THE SELF.. 114
Meditation for Relaxation *117*
Meditation for Visualization *119*
Meditation for Pain Relief *122*
Building Your Meditative Rhythm *125*

CONCLUSION 127

THE OLD AND THE NEW 129
What Next? *133*

REFERENCES 135

Introduction

For many people, the most fulfilling part of the healing process is finding their strength along the way. By harnessing your own natural ability to treat pain, discomfort, and anguish, you can learn to retake agency over your life. This element is often missing from westernized medicine, which focuses on the cure more than the journey. Of course, these methods are important to curing disease and injury, but are they fulfilling to the whole mind, body, and spirit? Do they repair the damage done to your energy, and better you for it?

Any ailment of modern society should be treated by a medicinal doctor and complementary, holistic practice. It is not enough to simply mend the body, and move on with your life as if everything is back to normal. When you have dealt with a significant struggle, your spirit has been weakened along the way. With a diminished spirit, you may face traces of your struggle again later in life, or things that hold you back in your daily routines.

This guide serves to supplement its sister book, *Sacred Woman*, also by Kara Lawrence. Whether you are a woman yourself, or anyone else seeking out the healing feminine touch, *Spiritual Medicine* is your step-by-step companion along your holistic journey. The methods outlined in the following chapters contain techniques to heal ailments of the mind, body, and spirit, and strengthen the bonds between them for a better, complete sense of self. By using inherent elements of the spirit, anyone can harness the rejuvenating forces of their own feminine energy.

Kara speaks from her own experience throughout this guide, providing instructional information on holistic techniques she has found to be approachable, fulfilling, and inspiring during her journey. She will take you through a variety of different techniques with different targets, each providing a particular kind of relief, relaxation, or revival. This can help you find the right approach for your personal spiritual needs, and finesse the practice that fits into your schedule.

What to Expect

In this guide, Kara covers all the basics of starting your own holistic self-healing practice. She provides insight on her perspective, and details on traditional spiritual concepts. In Chapters 1 and 2, you will learn the holistic definition of healing, and an in-depth look into how it harnesses spiritual energy. These concepts are explained upfront, reviewing the history, meaning, and context of them within alternative medicine. You will understand the fundamentals of using spiritual energy and holistic healing techniques before getting into the nitty gritty details later on. This means that you will come away from this book, not only with tried and true examples of how to utilize spiritual healing, but wielding the foundational knowledge that you need in order to craft your own new experiences.

The rest of *Spiritual Medicine* is dedicated to providing insight on techniques used to heal the mind, body, and spirit, each individually specialized for focusing on a particular element of health. You will discover the relationship the mind, body, and spirit have with energy flow, chakras, and vibration. Then, you'll be provided with a variety of different ways to strengthen *your* relationship with them as well.

These include, but are not limited to, acupressure, breathwork, aromatherapy, crystal healing, visualization exercises, daily affirmations, Reiki, and more. Each chapter will go in depth about the variations and usage of these techniques, and then provide step-by-step example exercises for you to utilize them at home. With this guide, you should be able to run your own practice, or use the information provided to seek out a healing professional or holistic community.

At the end of the book, Kara has dedicated the final chapter to several unique, guided meditations. These are meditations you can use at home, by yourself, for a variety of purposes. Each meditation contains suggestions for an intention you can set for the exercise, steps to perform it, and complementary healing components you could incorporate. You'll also get a few hints and tricks to creating a better environment for more productive meditation and healing practice.

Your Self and Yourself

Ultimately, the takeaway of *Spiritual Medicine* should be robust and fruitful. Not only will you find an abundance of new things to try, repeat, and enjoy during your spiritual healing, but you will also find a new appreciation for the person you are healing. That's you, by the way.

While you learn new ways of soothing, strengthening, and stimulating your natural energetic flow, you will also be building towards a better recognition of who you are. The best part of holistic medicine is that many parts of it can be done completely by yourself, allowing you to take agency over your own health, and find control over your life in the process. Even practices that require a professional to assist you (i.e. massage, Reiki, etc.) hinge upon your connection to the spirit, and the energetic potential you can bring to each session.

When Kara talks about "you" or "yourself," she wants to make sure what that means is clear. The Self, as an entity, is not simply your body, your brain, or your actions. It's all of these things, and so much more. You and your Self are powerful avatars of your inner spirit. You can heal many ailments by treating them with medicine, getting a procedure, or talking with a psychologist. These are completely valid ways of healing that will certainly bring an amount of relief to your day-to-day problems. Alternative medicine, however, serves to complement these treatments by harnessing that energetic potential hidden within you.

That's your Self. That's who you truly are, and sometimes that Self needs its own special healing.

Without you, alternative medicine is simply a collection of relaxing exercises that can bring calm to anyone's life. For some people, that's enough, and they may find it beneficial to use these methods simply for the sake of relaxation. For others, holistic practice finds a path from your outer awareness of your mind and body, inside towards the core of your being. This core holds not only your spirit, but your experiences, your loves and hates, your dreams and fantasies, your connections to others, and much more.

These invisible concepts are hard for many people to wrap their minds around. While they can understand the importance of things like intuition or identity, they aren't out in the open. It's hard to notice when something is struggling if you refuse to acknowledge that it is an extant, constant object in the universe. Something does not need to be physically present in order to be real.

By turning inward, you are acknowledging these truths. You will look deep within yourself to see the things that make you tick, and learn to check in with them more regularly. This process allows the Self to grow and thrive, and gives you opportunities to heal it when the time comes.

Further Reading

If you are interested in holistic healing, and find the techniques laid out in this book to be up your alley, you may consider looking into our sister guide *Sacred Woman*. It goes over the history, significance, and spiritual meaning behind many of the methods laid out in *Spiritual Medicine,* while also focusing on the importance of feminine spirituality. For spiritual women, loved ones of spiritual women, or anyone who wishes to get in touch with their own femininity, this book highlights the intrinsic connection to the female spirit and holistic health.

Chapter 1:

True Healing

In the media, holistic healing techniques are often misrepresented. We spiritual folk are no strangers to being called hippies, loonies, or wackos for being involved in spiritual medicine. Furthermore, many concerned populations portray alternative methods as a strictly unscientific approach to healing, and criticize those who choose to use them to better their lives. These ideas come from ignorance more often than hatred, but they still create a negative environment for those who want to use holistic therapy openly.

For anyone that hears about alternative medicine from one of these ignorant sources, it makes sense that they may want to speak up on the subject. Myths about this topic may cause people to think of holistic healing as a hoax, or a rejection of westernized medicine. This can lead people to be concerned for your health if they believe you might reject important medical treatments, or give all your money to a "fake" healer. Anyone who truly believes these myths has every reason to be worried for you if they don't know the truth.

So what about these misconceptions? Many of them come from a fear of the eccentric, and more are rooted in confusion. The core issue behind these problems comes from how we, as a culture, define "healing."

From a holistic perspective, healing is about more than mending wounds and curing disease. This difference is the key reason why many uneducated people dismiss alternative medicine as "fake," since it does not target the same problems as western medicine. The truth of the matter is that healing can have more than one meaning, and each has its own roots in fact.

One false belief that comes out of this confusion is the idea that holistic healers are untrained or scam artists. People who believe that anyone marketing themselves as a "healer" should be a medical doctor, which is simply not the case when you look at other definitions of healing. This reinforces the idea that all natural medicine practice is unscientific, and has no basis in evidence. Assumptions like this are extremely harmful to communities who practice these arts and benefit from them, and they are not true.

To be a licensed naturopathic doctor—as in, an individual who can prescribe treatments, and practice traditional medicine as an accredited professional—someone must go through four years of regulated schooling in order to run a legitimate practice. Anyone that claims to be a medical practitioner of holistic arts has studied the scientific facts behind natural medicine, and received a degree in the field (AANMC, 2020). This field is not made up of individuals with no experience or education; it is led by those who are just as educated as any other professional.

Other holistic healers may not be a licensed physician or hold a degree, but these practitioners rarely claim otherwise. To provide energy healing, massage therapy, or other spiritual medicine, someone does not have to be doing so in a clinical capacity. Many of those who offer these services make it clear that this is an exercise to provide healing in a holistic sense, and do not make false claims about curing cancer or paralysis. Charlatans who claim to do these things with alternative medicine are, in fact, scam artists, but do not represent the vast majority of the holistic community.

In fact, most legitimate holistic healers are not anti-medicine at all. Professional naturopaths and other accredited members of the traditional medicine community are educated in the purpose behind prescription medications, treatments, and therapies (AANMC, 2020). When seeing a patient, part of a medical naturopath's job is to assess the needs of a patient and recommend treatment based on where they are in the healing process. This can include prescribing medication, referring them to a specialist, or other practices within western medicine.

The idea that spiritual medicine rejects "reality" in favor of holistic practice is completely false. Most healers, as physicians, therapists, or self-taught, view spiritual medicine as a complementary treatment. This means that the methods used within these exercises are intended to pair alongside other medical treatments, or supplement the healing process afterwards. In many cases, holistic healing treats non-medical issues that relate to the spiritual health of the individual, not their body or mind.

Whatever the case, those who practice spiritual medicine do so in order to engage with holistic healing of the self. This means focusing on healthy energy flow, internal alignment, and wholeness. Ailments that are healed by these practices are completely different from those that are treated with medication, surgery, or therapy.

By comparing them, and refusing to acknowledge this difference, critics are misrepresenting a field they do not understand. It is easy to mock alternative medicine when the mainstream opinion of it is based on lies and bad examples. The fact of the matter is that, since the dawn of humankind, people have sought out healing in multiple forms. Ancient civilizations engaged more actively with spiritual medicine, and have identified the difference between medical and holistic treatments throughout time.

The Long History of Spiritual Healing

Humans have been trying to solve the art and science of healing since the Prehistoric era. Alongside learning to hunt, cook, craft, and build shelter, treating pain and discomfort were some of the first things we focused on as a species. Our natural ability to solve problems is what sets us apart from apes and other intelligent animals. People use tools and create new ideas in order to make their lives better; it's only natural that some of the earliest recorded humans were already trying to improve their own health.

Records from some of the earliest civilizations of Indigenous Africans and Aboriginal Australians show that these ancient cultures had a deep connection to spiritual health. These communities identified the spirit as an important part of an individual's life and purpose, and that problems within that spirit could reflect outwards into physical or mental symptoms.

Indigenous cultures dated back to 50,000-75,000 years ago hold stock in using holistic healing techniques alongside medical practice, finding many ailments had root in their version of "the spirit world" (Callaghan, 2017). In the modern era, today's Aboriginal groups still practice spiritual medicine alongside more contemporary techniques, seeing them as equally important parts of whole-body health. Healers in these groups often give credit to ancestors or mentors in the community, citing a long tradition of handing knowledge down to future generations. Because of this, the same holistic techniques being used in the present day can be traced back to these ancient ways.

Many other native tribes around the world used holistic techniques in their cultural tradition throughout history. In the Americas, indigenous groups used spiritual based therapy and herbal medicine in their healing. Native American tribes were highly advanced civilizations with hundreds of different cultures and beliefs. A common theme among them was a sophisticated understanding of using herbs and plants to relieve pain, treat infection, and soothe other ailments of the mind and body. Prominent medicine women and men would even use natural mixtures as remedies that predate their prescription version today (Callaghan, 2017).

Spirituality is the main difference between these herbal medications as used in modern medicine and their origins in Native American culture. For healers in these tribes, the spiritual aspect could not be removed from the practice of medicine without weakening the process. Using masks and paint to engage with spirits was common for healers, in order to ward off negative energy and invite positive presences into their practice. Using meditative chants, dances, and smokes to cleanse an area and connect with the spirit world was another common element used by healers during this time (Callaghan, 2017). When someone needed help, they were given treatment for their mind, body, and soul, and every environmental factor was considered relevant. This is a prime example of spiritually sensitive healers utilizing a holistic perspective in some of our oldest civilizations.

Similarly, doctors in Ancient Egyptian civilization tied their medical practice to holistic spiritualism in many ways. Divine beings such as deities, demons, and abstract spirits were thought to have a role in causing sickness and other health issues. Furthermore, despite having no relation to Hinduism or their concept of chakras, Ancient Egyptian healers believed that energetic channels could be blocked by negative spiritual energies, causing health and lifestyle issues (Callaghan, 2017). Understanding these channels led them to learn about physical structures of the skeleton and human organs.

Much of today's understanding of holistic healing theory comes from elements of traditional Chinese medicine. This form of medicinal practice is considered to be the third oldest form of healing in the world, dating back thousands of years to Ancient Chinese cultures.

Traditional Chinese medicine centers around four basic tenets, the first of which being that the human body mirrors that of the universe. This means that it represents a smaller ecosystem of its own needs, just like the world around it. The second tenet is represented by yin and yang, the two opposing forces of nature. The constant balance of these forces brings harmony to the world, while an imbalance can lead to turmoil, disease, and other problems. Third, is the concept of the elements. In traditional Chinese medicine, these are earth, wood, fire, metal, and water, and they represent an aspect of all things, including the stages of human life (Callaghan, 2017).

The final tenet of this practice is the concept of Qi. Ancient Chinese healers used Qi as a representation of the spiritual energy that moves through all of us (Callaghan, 2017). It can serve many different functions, and brings a balance of positive and negative forces through our mind, body, and spirit.

In contemporary holistic healing, practitioners around the world use elements of traditional Chinese medicine in their spiritual exercises. These have been passed down since the dawn of modern medicine, and are used in different forms around the world. This is just one more example of holistic concepts being tried and true, finding a place in various forms of healing practice.

By looking further down the line, we can see this trend continues throughout the development of human civilization. This is no coincidence. Historians find examples of holistic methodology used in the Incas and Aztecs, Ancient Greek and Rome, traditional Indian culture, and even Medieval medicine (Callaghan, 2017). Even as we become more and more technologically advanced and scientifically minded, ideas of the spirit, energetic forces, and natural elements continue to play key roles in the healing arts.

Spiritual and medical practices have always been used in tandem, across vastly different cultures and time periods. These inseparable subjects have always benefited from being used together, and complement each other for the service of their people. When a healer focuses only on the body, and not on the individual's emotions, environment, experience, or energy, they are not using a holistic method. This can cut the healing process short, and limit the full potential of the practitioner's help.

Healing Holistically

This guide is designed for beginners and experienced healers alike. Many people starting out with spiritual medicine may have a hard time juggling all of the new terminology and concepts being thrown at them. You may ask, what's the difference between spiritual medicine and alternative medicine? What about traditional medicine? And what exactly does holistic mean? These are good questions, whether this is your first time hearing them, or you've been wondering for years.

Spiritual, alternative, and traditional are all words used to cover the broad umbrella of holistic practices. They can be used interchangeably, or more specifically if you're focusing on a particular aspect of the methodology in context. For example, spiritual medicine is often used when focusing on the energetic and spirit-based parts of the practice. Alternative and traditional medicine still encompass those aspects, but may be used when comparing it to westernized medicine, or trying to use a familiar term to outsiders.

The term "holistic" covers all of these bases, and can always be used in the same way. In some cases, I prefer to use the word holistic when talking about my healing process, and explaining the techniques to others. This is because I feel that it is the most descriptive of the healing process, and helps me to clarify the intent behind our healing exercises. Some people are put off by the term "spiritual medicine," because it falsely leads them to believe that this is an inherently religious experience. The word holistic refers to the treatment of the whole person. This means it focuses on the health of an individual from all sides, including social, mental, spiritual, and environmental factors.

Using holistic and explaining this definition allows people to see the true intent behind this type of healing. While spiritual and traditional approaches are equally significant in the community, holistic ideals are what makes this type of healing stand out from other techniques. Many of those who hold misconceptions about the nature of spiritual medicine will understand it better after learning the intent behind holistic practice.

More Than Medicine

The philosophy behind holistic and spiritual medicine relies upon a multi-angled perspective. This type of healing is not limited to injury, illness, and disorder, but it can aid in relieving symptoms of those things. Holistic practitioners understand that any given individual is made up of several interconnected parts. In order to treat that individual, you must be ready to treat each of those parts and the connections between them. This is the core belief that drives spiritual medicine.

Despite common belief, many practitioners of holistic healing provide a variety of health care services. Spiritual practices like energy healing, cleansing, and breathwork are all a part of holistic health, but these same healers may also prescribe medicine, recommend physicians, or provide psychotherapy, if certified (Hitti, 2011). There is nothing anti-healthcare about holistic healing, it simply focuses on the whole self instead of specializing in the body alone.

Holistic ideology promotes the belief that all people have a natural ability to heal (Hitti, 2011). This could come from spiritual connection, energetic flow, or innate power, depending on your perspective. To heal the whole self, you have to get in touch with your own healing forces and use them to drive the process. If some part of you doesn't want to get better, you won't have all the resources you need to be completely healthy, and you may handicap yourself along the way.

Practitioners of spiritual medicine also operate under the strict principle of viewing their patients as people first, not their condition (Hitti, 2011). This means that you or your healer should always be checking in with every part of you when beginning the healing process. Your emotions, mental state, physical comfort, and recent life changes are all important parts of a holistic check-up. When trying to heal your whole self, you must remember that these things affect your health more than you might expect.

Along the same lines, holistic practice doesn't just look at the symptoms or the underlying physical illness. These things are important to treat, obviously, but they are not the full picture. You want to make sure that the root cause of your problems is also being looked at during the healing process (Hitti, 2011). This may be a bad habit you have that exacerbates the issue, or a relationship in your life that keeps you from treating yourself right. Whatever it may be, that cause can often be examined and remedied through introspective, spiritual exercises.

These principles drive anyone who runs a professional holistic healing practice, but they are equally important for your self-driven exercises. When you use spiritual medicine at home, you should be treating yourself the same way you would expect to be treated by a naturopathic doctor. You should bring respect, understanding, and full attention to each healing exercise, and make sure that you look at yourself as the whole, complete person you are.

Repetition and Reinforcement

One unique advantage of holistic healing practice comes from the long-term nature of most methods. Within westernized medicine, many treatments involve a short procedure, a period of time on medication, or continued renewal of necessary prescriptions. When treatments target your energetic health, environmental influence, and other holistic focused parts of your life, they may require consistent upkeep in order to have a lasting effect.

For example, many newbies to spiritual medicine may try out meditation for the first time and feel like it was a total waste. This is not an uncommon situation—not because meditation is unpleasant, but because it doesn't immediately fix every problem. Meditation, like other introspective exercises, is about looking into yourself, learning something new, and using that to take the next step. Sometimes those steps can be small, but with enough repetition, you'll walk a long way.

This can make it hard to know if you like a certain exercise after the first time you try it. If you're interested in a technique, or think it may help you, get through it a few times on a regular schedule before making a final call. Approaching your holistic practice as part of your routine is an important part of measuring its success. Many techniques will only make a noticeable change over time, since spiritual healing is a soft, gradual artform.

Once you know something is working for you, the reinforcement comes into play. By using holistic healing, you are addressing multiple parts of your life that may be related to your overall health. Unless you want to make some huge changes, you aren't going to want to change everything about yourself in order to feel better. Instead, you want to find the parts of your life you are willing to change, and use spiritual medicine to reinforce healthier habits.

This may mean that you've identified a consistent problem in your life that can be treated with more exercise. Working out on its own hasn't been enough for you, so you've decided to incorporate spiritual yoga into your routine in order to connect your physical exercise with your energetic balance. Complementing the act of exercising with a spiritual focus can help you stay motivated, and add an intent to your routine. While becoming more physically healthy, you may also find a new relationship with your body, your emotions, or your purpose in life. Connecting these ideas can help you realize how each component of your life is related, and use one to reinforce the growth of another.

You don't have to see immediate results to know a holistic practice is serving a purpose in your life. If you enjoy it, and it brings you some form of peace, relief, or even entertainment, that is enough justification to incorporate it into your life. Your spirit drives your desires, so the simple act of wanting to continue a certain exercise means it is doing something to rejuvenate it.

Chapter 2:

Spiritual Energy and You

When approaching holistic concepts for the first time, some people may find that the concept of the spirit is harder to grasp than the rest. Caring for the mind and the body are ideas that are familiar enough to most people, but they are only two of the three core elements of holistic wholeness. The spirit, and what it represents, can mean many different things to different people. This is because of the very nature of what the spirit is, and how it can take form based on your personal perspective.

If you aren't religious, you may be initially turned off by the idea of embracing something labeled as "spiritual." This word often gets thrown around to go along with specific faiths. People with a strong relationship to Christianity or Judaism may call themself spiritual, while others may associate the word with ghosts or witchcraft. None of these definitions are necessarily wrong, but they don't quite fit into the holistic representation of what the spirit is. They certainly don't represent every side of the concept.

Alternative medicine and other holistic communities define the spirit as an innate force of energy that inhabits and connects all living things. For some, this can be a version of a deity, whether it be a god, goddess, or several, and it can be your soul. For others, it can represent an abstract power that provides protection, guidance, or purpose. Whatever your personal viewpoint is, that relationship between you and the spirit is what puts intent into your spiritual practice.

Traditionally, the idea of the spirit is represented through what we know of it in the physical and metaphysical world. While some disciplines define it differently than others, there is an underlying force to all things that drives humans to find meaning in it.

Within spiritual medicine, this is represented through energy, balance, and the inner self. These concepts are agnostic of any particular faith, and can fit into the broader relationship you may have with religion or science. The way you engage with positivity and negativity, and how it affects your life from within, is not represented purely through the body or the mind. That is where this third element of the spirit comes into play, to represent these less tangible parts of being a living, feeling, human being.

This chapter will cover several existing attitudes towards the spirit that exist within the broader holistic community. These may have aspects in common, and ones that contradict with one another; this is no mistake. Many practitioners of naturopathic arts and spiritual medicine embrace the identity of the spirit as fluid, and constantly changing. This is intrinsic to its nature as the most flexible part of us, controlling our compassion, our confidence, and our sensitivity. These softer, feminine traits of the spirit allow it to take many forms depending on the needs you may have in your life at any given time.

If the spirit makes the most sense to you as an embodiment of your personal soul, let that guide your relationship with healing by reflecting upon that inner self and embracing its communication with you. Maybe you are more interested in the spirit as an energetic force, constantly flowing within your channels. Then you may use spiritual healing to cleanse and find balance in your life. Finally, if the emotional element of the spirit strikes you as the most significant, it's possible that your sense of meaning in life is lacking, and the spirit is fighting from within to lead you towards a higher purpose.

Take time to learn about different ways holistic communities around the world embrace the spirit into their practice and allow yourself to project on the subject. Listen to your gut instincts, and pay attention to what your unconscious latches onto. These little signs are your spiritual energy sparking, and finding a connection to particular ideas. This may mean you are simply interested in them, but it may mean that they hold a special meaning to what your spirit is starved for. Listen to the needs of your mind, body, and spirit as a whole, especially if you don't quite understand what that looks like yet.

The Many Spirits

The concept of the spirit can represent different things, but it exists within all of us regardless. Most people can agree that we are more than just our flesh and brainpower; it's what fills that void that changes across communities. Historically, humans have conceptualized the spirit in the form of an inner soul, a presence in the afterlife, and a connection to nature, among other things. These ideas draw significance to the lives of those who hold them, and that significance drives them to lead better lives.

This is where the unified spiritual ideal comes into play with holistic medicine. When healing the whole, integrated self, the spirit cannot be ignored, no matter what it represents to you. Spiritual medicine relies on that sense of significance to draw positive energy into your life, and uses it throughout the healing process. This is where spirituality and religion find their separation, while still able to be used together if you so choose to.

It is vital that you understand this core principle when engaging with holistic practice. Let's look at a few definitions of spirituality from academic sources on the topic, and see what they have in common.

Wanda K. Mohr describes spirituality in her article *Spiritual Issues in Psychiatric Care,* as "a person's experience of, or a belief in, a power apart from his or her own existence" (Mohr, 2006). Conversely, in *Religion, spirituality, and health care: Social, ethical, and practical considerations* by Alan Astrow et al., spirituality is defined as, "the search for transcendent meaning" and that it "can be expressed in religious practice or . . . expressed exclusively in their relationship to nature, music, the arts, a set of philosophical beliefs, or relationships with friends and family" (Astrow et al., 2001).

My favorite definition comes from a medical essay entitled *Spirituality and the Physician Executive: Reconciling the Inner Self and the Business of Health Care,* by Leland Kaiser, where this broadness is defined rather poignantly. Kaiser writes, "Spirituality is about the relationship between ourselves and something larger. That something can be the good of the community or the people who are served by your agency or school or with energies greater than ourselves. Spirituality means being in the right relationship with all that is. It is a stance of harmlessness toward all living beings and an understanding of their mutual interdependence" (Kaiser, 2000).

These are only a few examples of intellectual theory in the field of spirituality, wherein it becomes clear that the spirit, even in terminology alone, is fluid and full of robust interpretation. This flexibility centers around finding purpose, connecting to inner and higher powers, and being at peace with the world around you.

There are common ways this shows up in modern and ancient spiritual dogma. They tend to fall into three broad thematic categories: the soulful, energetic, and emotional. Again, these theories have a lot in common, and you can draw from all or none of them in your practice. What matters is that you find an approach that fulfills your personal needs.

The Soulful Spirit

Frequently, people associate the term "spirit" with ghosts, angels, and other images of the deceased. This is due, not only to the prevalent belief in an afterlife, but also the idea of an innate human soul. Studies show that over 80% of Americans believe that the human soul exists after bodily death. The amount of Americans that think an afterlife exists for their spirit has increased gradually since 1972, even though the amount who identify as "religious" has decreased (Fox, 2016). This trend highlights the broad appeal of the soulful spirit ideology.

Those who believe in the human soul often believe in its innate power as a celestial or metaphysical part of you. This approach is used in Christian, Jewish, and Muslim dogma, among other mainstream religions. Many people who do not identify as members of these religions still find comfort in the idea of having a soul, or some amount of spiritual energy that represents who they are as a sentient person, and may last well beyond their death.

This can also be seen in religions like Buddhism and Hinduism, which represent the soul through the idea of reincarnation. While it doesn't describe the afterlife as a concrete location, it emphasizes the longevity of the soul, and its place in a larger cycle of spiritual energy. Depending on the particular discipline, these faiths may describe reincarnation as part of an eternal, energetic balancing act, or as a result of karmic justice. In any case, the idea that there is an inner spiritual force that inhabits all of us prevails within these religions as well.

When participating in holistic practice, you may find that this understanding of the spirit appeals to you the most. Meditation, crystal healing, Reiki, and other spiritual exercises may invite you to conceptualize your spirit within your mind, and make communication with it. By visualizing your spirit as your inner self, or your soul, you can find that core energy that connects you with your place here on earth.

Whether that is a part of an eternal reincarnation cycle, a trial before your transition to the afterlife, or simply the internal essence that drives you through this earth, this soul is an important part of your identity. It encapsulates your power, your purpose, and your intent. By finding a connection to it, you are finding a connection to the core of your being. This connection serves to bring energy to and from that soul, and uses it to heal your whole mind, body, and spirit.

The Energetic Spirit

Another way of looking at spiritual medicine is through the lens of energetic theory. This does not directly contradict a soul-based outlook, and can even enhance or complement it when understanding the spirit. Though, if you find yourself unfulfilled by these representations, the energetic model is highly applicable to many forms of practice.

The core tenet behind spiritual energy therapy is that everything is made up of a set of fundamental, invisible forces. Those forces create the energy that drives creation, growth, connection, and life throughout the universe. In an era where we are discovering new galaxies, parallel worlds, and infinite stars, it's hard to ignore the fact that energy is everywhere. The natural reaction for many people is to find synchrony with that energy, and tap into it to better understand their lives.

Within spiritual medicine, this force is seen as another form of the spirit. When everything around us is made up of energy, humans are therefore, ultimately, balls of that same energy. This energy is potent, and can be affected by the energy of things around us. This can affect the health of your spirit, depending on the balance of positive and negative energy influences in your life, and things that may be blocking the flow of your spiritual channels.

Imagine, for a moment, that you are a teapot. In order to be a functional, "happy" teapot, you should be able to make tea. The water that comes out of the tap is like the flow of spiritual energy coming into you from the outside. When you ask for it, that water fills you up, and you can start the tea-making process. Then, you need heat. As the energy of heat is added to the equation, the teapot uses its natural insulation to warm the water and bring it to a boil. That's how your inner channels harness that spiritual energy and process it into what you need. If all goes well, you'll be able to pour that hot water out and over your teabag, and the natural elements of the tea will combine with what you made to make something completely new.

This metaphor represents a basic understanding of energy flow within your spirit. By welcoming in water (energy from outside elements) and adding your own heat to it (energy from within yourself), you create a new balanced force that can be used to drive creation, purpose, and motivation in your day-to-day life.

During this process, the water you took in will separate into two components. Some of it will stay as water, and be used to make your tea. The rest will evaporate into steam. If you don't release the steam from the teapot in time, it will begin to whistle, and eventually it may build up pressure and cause everything to bubble over. Think of this when we discuss unbalanced energies in later sections of the guide. If you find yourself with too much negativity or positivity, it may build up inside of you and form blockages. This can cause your body and mind to be flushed with overflowing energy bursts at times, or deprived of energy when they need it most. Many common ailments have roots in these problems.

Furthermore, what if the water is tainted to begin with? Pouring dirty water into a teapot won't produce good tea. By acknowledging the spirit as an energetic force, you are acknowledging that your spirit can be affected by toxicity and bad vibrations. Sometimes, your spirit may need to be cleansed, or even revived during the healing process in order to realign the balance within your channels.

By acknowledging that the very same energy flowing through us also flows through others, through nature, and back into ourselves again, we can embrace this cycle to find new sources of power. Spiritual energy is like breathing with your whole self. This means taking in the energy that is best for you, and sending it back out into the world after you're done with it.

Holistic practice relies on the theory that everything is a part of a larger whole, whether it's your mind, body, and spirit, or you, your peers, and the earth itself. This means that your individual spiritual energy makes up a part of a larger flow. You can tap into this larger pool of energy by finding spiritual connections to your environment, peers, or inner self.

The Emotional Spirit

The final perspective I wanted to share in this section views the spirit as a purely emotional, internal concept, driven by a sense of higher purpose. When you find yourself feeling lost, listless, or pointless, you may associate this with the mind alone. Mental disorders, unfortunate circumstances, and chronic pain are a few things that can elicit these problems in life. The holistic perspective invites us to embrace these truths, while still connecting them back to problems within the spirit.

No antidepressant or extra vitamin will fill the void of a meaningless life. They may help with your day-to-day struggles, and give you relief during the process, but that is not all there is to the healing process. Many individuals with perfectly healthy minds and bodies still struggle to imbue their lives with fulfilling ideals. They may feel that being comfortable day-to-day is proof that life is pointless, and that their contentedness loses value over time.

This is an indicator of a spiritually unhealthy person. For those that aren't interested in the idea of a soul, afterlife, or energetic cycle, many find that using spiritual medicine still resonates with them on an emotional level for this reason. Taking control over your view of the world, and of yourself, is an exercise in self-discipline and mindfulness.

Some individuals find that changing your perspective on life is easy. Others find that this is challenging without some sort of underlying structure or dogma driving them to look at things a different way. For this type of person, using the spirit as an ideological touchstone can be extremely helpful.

Western thought circles often try to separate things into separate, conflicting forces. The idea that dark is always the enemy of light, or that fire must always fight with water is something ever-present in the way our culture views the world. This can breed unfortunate consequences in our mind, body, and spirit, as we begin to separate things and put them against each other without an acknowledgment for the greater whole. For this reason, many people hold a false perspective about their place in the world.

Spiritual medicine focuses on the holistic alternative to these ideals. For example, a shadow cannot exist without the sun's shine, and a flame can combine with water to create steam that powers trains. This change in perspective is intrinsic to contemporary spirituality, and emphasizes the connectedness between all elements of the universe.

By engaging with holistic practice, you are getting in touch with that spiritual connection by changing your outlook on the world. Using meditation, affirmation, and other spiritual techniques can help you become more mindful about these things. Introspective practices can help you get in touch with your inner self and project itself outward, allowing you to harness that spiritual motivation to manifest your hopes and desires.

Energy and Balance

Whether or not you believe that your energetic aura is the same thing as the spirit, holistic medicine relies on a general understanding of it. From the rocks beneath our feet to the stars above our heads, everything around us is made up of energy in one way or another. This includes us, ultimately, as fundamentally energetic beings. We are filled with this force the same way that the universe is filled with light and matter. This means that we are also a part of a larger balancing cycle, and we can be channels for energy ourselves.

Energy medicine is being acknowledged more and more in health science today. The fact that there are unseen forces that interact with our day-to-day lives is the core principle of energetic medicine and distant healing theory. It offers the idea that there are certain vibrations, channels, and alignments that affect our perception of the world, and those can be manipulated for healing purposes. Holistic practitioners use this science directly, by working with chakras, sounds, crystals, and more, to affect the energetic aura of their patients. These ideas are used more indirectly within western medicine, but their use is on the rise nonetheless.

The difference between these two communities tends to be about their central focus. Westernized medicine works more with physical and mental treatments, while holistic medicine aims to strengthen the interconnectedness of the whole self. What many people fail to realize is that these can work in conjunction, complementing one another.

We see this highlighted with the increased use of energetic and distant healing. In mainstream medical practices, the use of light therapy has been shown to relieve symptoms of psoriasis (Silver, 2011). Light is one of the most visible forms of energy to human beings. It is used in our daily lives, not only to help us see, but to alter moods, power technology, and create warmth. In its most basic form, this is a way that humans have harnessed intangible energy for the sake of bettering their lives.

Furthermore, there is presence of wavelengths beyond the field of human vision. These rays and waves are used frequently within medicine, through MRI scans and ultrasound machines (Silver, 2011). Because they have been practiced and proven within scientific communities, these are considered mainstream medical techniques, rather than alternative or traditional. That being said, they still fall into the broader field of energy medicine, when it comes down to it.

Holistically driven techniques are still frequently used to complement medical treatments and recovery periods within these same scientific circles. Energy healing techniques are frequently used to provide relaxation and stability to patients going through extensive physical therapy or recovering from a painful condition. Music therapy is another accepted technique used alongside treatment for physical and mental symptoms (Silver, 2011). This is done by harnessing the power of vibrational energy (sound) used in soothing, stimulating, or otherwise therapeutic ways for the patient's benefit. Whether used standalone or alongside another treatment, this is a form of energy healing.

By investing in these ideas and looking further into the benefits of harnessing energy for healing techniques, you are engaging in spiritual medicine. The same force that powers light and sound also flows through you. It is about the give and take between your self—the mind, body, and spirit of it—and the broader universe. These factors balance out onto an invisible scale, the state of which affects your spiritual health.

Think of it this way: even on your most average, normal day, there are a number of things that may affect how you feel. Your mental and physical health, of course, will drastically impact your emotional state in any situation. For the sake of this example, let's say that your mind and body are at the peak of healthiness. Even though it seems as if "nothing is wrong," you may still find yourself restless, bored, hyperactive, or any number of states that will completely change the course of the day. Why?

It may sound obvious, but it is in fact because of these energetic factors that constantly surround you. When you enter an extremely bright room, that light is going to affect you. It may fill you with energy or it may give you a headache, depending on the balance of energy already present within your system. Similarly, if you sit in a room with ambient, trance-inducing sounds, you may find yourself being coaxed into a tranquil state, or even exhausted. These are some straight-forward examples of how energetic forces can noticeably affect the way you experience life.

By practicing spiritual medicine, you can become an expert in the less straight-forward ways that this occurs. There are many theories on the way spiritual energy works and different techniques on how to harness it.

Most of these approaches do not contradict one another; they are merely meant to be a framework through which you can understand the abstract, invisible nature of energetic healing. We'll cover some of these perspectives here, but make sure that you work with what makes the most sense to you, first and foremost. If a particular viewpoint doesn't make sense to you, or you have your own special understanding of the relationship between energy and your spirit, then embrace it.

This philosophy is vital as you start your self-guided holistic practice. By taking charge of your own healing journey, you have the privilege of shaping how it looks. Many of the techniques outlined in this guide will help you utilize introspection and mindfulness to understand your needs. The act of turning inward is an integral part of most of these techniques, making it easy to learn new things about yourself, and try new approaches in the process.

Negative and Positive Energy

A common understanding of energetic health comes from the balancing act of negative and positive energy. Many spiritual healing exercises center around clearing negative presences and inviting positive energy into the system. This may be presented as part of chakra flow, or spiritual channels being blocked by overwhelming amounts of negativity or overstimulated by an imbalance of positivity. This theory ultimately hinges upon the idea of balance, so it is important to remember that both types of energy are necessary for a healthy spirit.

In general, positive energy may sound more appealing to most people. In today's world, the majority of spiritual ailments come from an oversaturation of negativity, whether it be from media, materialism, relationships, or other unavoidable influences (Scott, 2020). It is easier to identify when an excess of these negative things have caused a problem in your life, and determine the best course of action to cleanse them properly.

Some typical symptoms of negative spiritual energy are increased stress, demotivation, and pessimism. These can also be symptoms of a larger problem in your life, but the difference in this case is the perception of the negativity. When you find yourself experiencing more stress than you think is normal for your situation, that may be a sign that something is energetically unbalanced within you. This is most noticeable when your inner dialog with yourself is highly negative, filled with unnecessarily dark thoughts or habitual exaggeration of bad events (Scott, 2020). When everything feels like the straw that breaks the camel's back when it really isn't, there's something abnormal happening.

If you feel like you are stuck in a rut, for whatever reason, you may have an abundance of negative energy that needs to be cleared from your spirit. There are a number of holistic exercises that you can use to get in touch with that energy, find its source, and replace it with something better. These will be discussed in later chapters for your benefit, but feel free to experiment with anything that allows you to introspect and practice mindfulness over your inner thoughts. This is the root of many spiritual exercises, as it allows you to talk back to that negative force and separate it from your identity.

Similarly, you can run into a number of health problems related to an oversaturation of positive energy. It might sound weird, but even within spiritual energy there can be too much of a good thing. In most cases, positive energy is a way to generate a healthy flow within your channels and influence personal growth and fulfillment. If you find yourself regularly overstimulated, or restless, you may have an imbalance somewhere within your chakras. This doesn't mean that you should invite negative energy into your life; instead, you should get in touch with the alignment of your spirit. There could be a blockage somewhere within your chakras or spiritual channels, causing positive energy to build up with nowhere to go. Think of it like a clog in the system, keeping things from flowing correctly.

Exercises that focus on cleansing, realigning, and balancing your energetic center are great for dealing with these types of problems (Scott, 2020). You might find that you have difficulty sitting still, focusing on tasks, or feeling satisfied. These can be caused by all of that positive energy sitting around in one part of you, building up more and more. In the worst-case scenario, this can cause outbursts, reckless decisions, or erratic behavior, when that pocket of energy finally bursts.

Alignment

Another key concept in the world of spiritual energy healing is the idea of being in alignment. This can have a few meanings, depending on context, but it ultimately comes back to the core intent behind holistic medicine. In order to be spiritually healthy, you want your mind, body, and spirit to be aligned with each other, and for your energies within to be aligned in the same way. This can manifest differently depending on how you visualize your spiritual energy, how you like to work with it, and the relationship you have with your mind and body.

The fundamentals of holistics require a strong relationship between the mind, body, and spirit in order to be completely healthy. This relationship emphasizes a healthy bond between each element, and open pathways for energy to flow. In some cases, you may find holistic health issues that stem from those paths being blocked or restricted from each other. In others, the paths might be twisted and damaged due to being out of alignment.

This means that your mind, body, and spirit are each doing their job independently, but they aren't working in synchrony with one another. As a result, your spiritual energy is going to have a harder time flowing from each element to the next, making you less whole over all. Over time, this can damage your relationship with yourself as a whole. Having a disconnect between the mind, body, and spirit may cause issues like poor body image, impulsive behavior, unhealthy eating decisions, and more (Rose, 2019). These potential issues crop up when one significant part of you isn't working in sync with the rest, causing it to feel less and less like something you should be nurturing healthily.

Many spiritual exercises focus on realigning these elements through awareness and consciousness. One example of this may involve accepting your emotions and learning to express them healthily, rather than bottling them up. Hiding your emotions can cause them to build up over time, and cause your mind to become misaligned. To fix this, you can draw your feelings out from your mind, and express them through your body. This could mean shouting into your pillow, dancing around like crazy, or using exercise to vent emotional energy (Rose, 2019). By using your physical form to get in touch with these emotions, you are bringing your mind and body back into synchrony together, creating a healthier balance between them.

Alignment is also important when it comes to your chakras. Within spiritual medicine, chakras represent the major energy crossroads within your spiritual channels. These are areas of highly concentrated spirit energy, such as intersections and central points of focus within your body. There are seven main chakras, each representing a significant part of your mind, body, and spirit, and their function in your life.

These major chakras run up your body through the center, similar to your spine (Lindberg, 2020). When energy flow is unbalanced, or filled with toxic influences, these chakras may become unhealthy. One way that this happens is due to misalignment.

The chakras are partially responsible for creating the channels through which your energy travels. When they are out of alignment, you may find that negative energy gathers in a particular area of your mind or body. This could manifest in the form of a particularly mysterious ache, or frequently unexplained stress (Lindberg, 2020). Whatever the symptom may be, these symptoms can be soothed through realigning the chakras. This will allow that excess of energy, or lack thereof, to be mended through the natural flow of the spirit within you.

Many holistic exercises focus on alignment in ways that are easy to grasp and incorporate into your daily practice. By using physical realignment exercises such as yoga, movement therapy, and massage, you can find alignment of the whole through the channel of the body (Rose, 2019). Since the mind, body, and spirit are all connected, using your body to promote realignment and healthy posture can reinforce the same through the mind and spirit. This is the strength of holistic practice, allowing you to use one part of yourself to promote health in the whole.

In this way, you can start with any familiar spiritual medicine exercise, and use it to find balance within. By finding healthy alignment in one aspect of your life, you may add exercises that bring in the rest. If you find that crystal therapy or Reiki is particularly fulfilling for you, bring it into your meditation, yoga, or aromatherapy as well.

When you combine techniques that benefit you, you are inviting natural synchrony into your routine. Letting your spirit move in tandem with your mind and body allows that chakra flow to open up and spread energy throughout your whole self. This can bring warmth, health, understanding, and awareness to parts of you that have been neglected for a long time.

Synchrony is Healing

The remaining chapters of this guide each focus on a particular element of holistic health. I have included some of my favorite spiritual medicine techniques, information about their purpose, and instructions on how to complete them. While each chapter highlights a particular category of spiritual medicine, concentrating on the mind, body, or spirit, I want to make sure that the flexibility of these methods is clear.

Exercises that work with the body directly can also benefit the mind and spirit, and the same can be said for the mental and spiritual practices included in the following chapters. These categories are for your benefit of understanding the channel through which energy is being used to heal you, not the symptoms it is healing. By utilizing bodywork, you will practice spiritual medicine through the channel of the body, using it as a tool.

Keep this in mind as we continue through this part of the guide. The most important part of using spiritual medicine is remembering that you are one, holistic, unified being. The best way to find your natural healing energy is to synchronize your mind, body, and spirit together, using the powers of each to strengthen the rest.

Chapter 3:

Channeling Through the Body

Some of the most popular techniques used within spiritual medicine use the body as the primary channel for healing energy. This is because many of our experiences as human beings come through the five senses, each of which are physical in nature. These sensations are what anchors many people to reality, allowing them to get in touch with new thoughts and feelings while focusing on the body.

Life is a glorious process full of moving parts and interlocking pieces. The role the body plays in this process is as a vessel, moving our minds and spirits through the world that we inhabit. Existing within the universe inspires sleeping, waking, talking, and walking. It brings us to build homes to shelter us from the storms above, and to gaze out the windows at them and marvel at their beauty. Humans have always held a deep reverence for the physical world, and our bodies are the portal through which we get to experience it.

Think of it like a ship at sea. The boat itself is the body, strong and beautiful, ready to travel across the ocean to its desired destination. It protects the captain and crew inside, and follows their map towards a greater importance. In this way, many might look upon this scene and believe that the boat does all the hard work. It weathers the storm, shields the people, and gets the job done... but can it work alone?

Without the crew inside, there is no one to steer the ship, or fuel it with energy. Without their direction, their map, and their goals, the ship would stay docked at shore with nowhere to go. This ship is a whole, functioning system with a powerful vessel, but a vital mind and spirit to make that body fulfill its purpose. In this same way, your own body is only as good as the health of your whole.

When taking care of your body, you want to prioritize the physical benefits of your practice just as much as the mental and physical ones. Using bodywork is about clearing and strengthening a channel for your energy to travel through, and properly nourish your whole system. By using mindful exercise, awareness therapy, and conscious breathwork, you can practice tying your physical health to your mental and spiritual well-being.

The methods highlighted in this chapter aim to accomplish exactly that. Through these techniques, you will first acknowledge your body, and open a dialog with it. Learning to pay attention to your unconscious actions, like breath, posture, and tension, helps you practice mindfulness about other aspects of your life. It can be easy to miss aches and pains after they become chronic, or undermine a discomfort in your life that could be eliminated with a little effort. If you take time to stop and listen to what your body is telling you, you may find that there is a lot to work on. Over time, this will help you become more attentive to the way your body affects your moods, goals, and lifestyle decisions too.

Bodywork Methods

In our overly-complicated lives, many of us learn the bad habit of moving in ways that are harmful to our bodies. It's easy to notice pain when it becomes severe, and treat it with medical care. By fixing injuries, strains, and other consequences of moving wrong, we often move on with our lives thinking it's over and done. In some cases, this may be true, but not always. More often than not, our bodies experience aches, tension, inflammation, irritation, and any number of other ailments due to the way we mistreat it day-to-day. Wouldn't it be nice to ease these problems before they culminate in a medical condition, or worse?

The goal of spiritual bodywork is to use holistic methods to increase awareness of the way we may be neglecting our bodily health. The way our lives are shaped around work and domesticity often encourages lifestyles that put us into unnatural contortions. One of the most common examples of this comes with posture, especially for those that work at a desk for long periods of time. Sitting in ways that clench our muscles, collapse our chests, and crunch our bones is not great for us in the long-run (Healthwise, 2019). These are not positions our bodies are meant to stay in for long periods of time, and without taking time to counteract this, we can suffer for this.

Other common symptoms of this casual body neglect can come from stress. For many of us, emotional turmoil, trauma, and trouble are unavoidable in life. Whether it's an environmental factor you can't control, a past experience, or a habit you haven't yet shaken, you may have a source of chronic stress in your life already. These problems are not always easily solved, and can cause further issues as a domino effect.

Frequent stress can cause back pain, joint pain, headaches, insomnia, high blood pressure, and even heart attacks, if untreated (Pietrangelo, 2020). This is one of the most obvious examples of the health of your mind and body being intrinsically connected. Most people experience stress at some point in their life. Whether it's over something you consider silly, or significant negative circumstances, it's going to have an effect on your body.

Bodywork uses the body as a conduit to address problems like this, moving backwards, from the symptom through to the source. If you can't wave a magic wand and eliminate the source of stress in your life, that's okay, a lot of people can't. What you can do, through spiritual bodywork, is learn to hack your body in order to calm your mind and spiritual energies. This has a double benefit for you, by using holistic exercises to relieve physical discomfort, and reduce the stress that may be making that discomfort worse.

While your body gets stronger, you may also find your mind is clearer, and your spirit more active. These benefits come from the power that inherently lives within your flesh, as you use it to its full potential.

If any of these exercises appeal to you, give them a try, and see how you can fit them into other holistic practices that you enjoy. The examples described in the following sections should be approachable to beginners, and easy to follow. After you try them a few times, you may find benefit in adding your own new steps, or integrating other techniques into the process. This is totally okay, and encouraged! This guide includes a sampling of the building blocks you need to dip your feet into the vast pool of spiritual medicine exercises. Whether you decide to jump in and swim to the other side is up to you; you may just be surprised what you find in the water along the way.

Acupressure and Reflexology

With roots in traditional Chinese medicine, acupuncture and acupressure are ancient techniques. In its original practice, acupressure therapists target channels of Qi, or life-force energy, with intense pressure, in order to stimulate it into motion and heal blockages (Rodriguez, 2016). For those that use acupuncture, needles are used on these same areas for a similar purpose. This section will focus primarily on acupressure, since it is more approachable to do at home, but they have the same core principles. Using a sharp needle untrained can pose potential risks regarding cleanliness and injury, so please consult a professional if you are more interested in trying the acupuncture method.

Acupressure is utilized by finding your natural spiritual channels, whether through Qi, chakra, or another type of energy. These exist at physical locations on your body, and can be learned with study and practice. By putting pressure onto these key points, you can activate the energy channels within you, and utilize them to direct energy flow to a certain part of your body.

This may be used to relieve pain, promote muscle relaxation, or even mobilize your immune system. Some acupressure work relies on single points of focus, pressed for sustained periods of time. Other, more advanced methods involve acupressure-based massage. What every acupressure technique has in common is the use of energetic pressure points. These can be divided into two categories, based on their purpose in the therapy: local points and trigger points.

Local pressure points are energetic centers on your body that are located directly where the symptom is occurring (Rodriguez, 2016). This may be the point of pain, tension, or illness that the therapist is trying to heal.

By targeting a pressure point on the part of the body that you are trying to heal, you can use acupressure techniques to stimulate the channels and bring healing energy towards it. In some cases, this could involve concentrated pressure to increase blood, warmth, and positive energy to the location, to relieve pain. In others, it may mean intense, localized massage, used to open up blocked channels and promote realignment in the affected area. These techniques use your natural energy closest to the point of pain, and activate its ability to heal you from within (Rodriguez, 2016).

Trigger pressure points operate on the same principle, but at indirect locations on other parts of your body (Rodriguez, 2016). This may be used if the area you're trying to heal is too sensitive to touch directly, or if blocked chakras are preventing the flow of energy through the necessary channels.

Since your body is a circuit-like network of energy, there is no beginning or end to the spiritual flow within you. Just like your bloodstream, there is a constant loop of channels and chakras, sending energy to each and every part of your body when it works correctly. For this reason, you can find places where these channels intersect, and energy is powerfully concentrated. Targeting these areas with acupressure can allow you to change the direction of the energy's flow, and send it towards the area of pain, even if it's on the other side of your body (Rodriguez, 2016).

Acupressure artists understand this network, and use their knowledge to highlight points where this is the most possible. Think of it like knowing the subway system in a big city. If you need to get downtown, and the shortest path is closed for construction, you might think there's no way to get there. By knowing the map of the subway, though, you might learn that you can take the long way around on another route, and still get there in time.

If you want a serious acupressure massage or acupuncture treatment, look for holistic practitioners in your area. Naturopaths that practice this art can perform sophisticated therapies to target a number of chronic ailments towards your mind, body, and spirit.

That being said, there is a lot you can do with acupressure at home. If you're more interested in trying it out for yourself, you can learn simple ways to implement it into your spiritual medicine practice. For certain common ailments, there are acupressure points you can memorize and determine how they might influence the rest of your body.

Major Acupressure Points

Please note: If you are pregnant, or prone to blood clots, some of these acupressure points may be unsafe to use (Fletcher, 2019). Consult your doctor or a professional before using acupressure on yourself if you meet either of these conditions. Additionally, if you are experiencing new symptoms involving intense pain or potential symptoms of a medical emergency, please see a doctor in order to determine if additional treatment may be needed for your symptoms. Acupressure should always be used for minor conditions or in tandem with additional health care.

Otherwise, feel free to experiment a little. This chart shows a few common pressure points that you can use to soothe a variety of symptoms. They are primarily located on your hand and wrist, where a large amount of concentrated energy channels intersect. There are many other locations on your body that can be used for acupressure purposes, but for home practice, the hand is the easiest place for beginners to access alone.

To use these points, find the location with the chart below. Use your other hand to press firmly on the location. It should be strong pressure, without cutting off blood circulation to any parts of your hand.

Name	Location	Purpose
Four Seams	Four spots, located on each finger, on the inside of the lowest joint.	Relieves digestive problems, stomach pain, and irritable bowels.
Ten Dispersions	Ten spots, located on the tips of each finger and thumb.	Relieves symptoms like fever or sore throat, often related to the flu.
Base of Thumb	One spot, located by tracing a line from your thumb, down your palm, to the crease of your wrist.	Relieves shortness of breath, respiratory discomfort, and other breathing problems.
Small Intestine 3	Located below the pinky finger, and above the first large crease in your palm.	Relieves pain from headaches, earaches, and neck problems.
Hand Valley	Located in the meaty part of your hand between the thumb and forefinger.	Relieves stress and tension, as well as pain in the teeth, shoulders, and neck.

Lung Meridian	Located as a line, going from the top of your thumb, down your palm, below the last crease of your wrist.	Rubbing sore spots in this area with firm pressure relieves sneezing, sore throat, chills, and other cold symptoms.
Heart 7, or Spirit Gate	Located by tracing a line from your pinky finger down to the bottom of your palm, and pressing just outside of the pointy bone in your wrist.	Relieves symptoms of insomnia, depression, and anxiety.
Outer Gate	Located on the top of your wrist, three fingers down from your palm, in the middle of your arm.	Relieves symptoms of lethargy, lack of motivation, and stimulates immune response.
Inner Gate	Located on the underside of your wrist, three fingers down from your palm, in the middle of your arm.	Relieves symptoms of nausea, digestive problems, and stomach irritation.

Data listed in the above chart was found in *Hand Pressure Points: Charts and Uses,* written by Jenna Fletcher for Medical News Today (Fletcher, 2019).

Yoga

Now, if you're looking for something a little more physical, there are a lot of easy ways to imbue spirituality into your daily exercise goals. Let's face it. In our comfortable, modern lives, most of us could stand to work out a little more. Even the fittest adults need consistent activity to maintain their physical health and mental well-being. You may or may not have an exercise routine already, but if you're interested in holistic bodywork, spiritual yoga is an easy way to get the best of both worlds.

There's a good chance that you may have tried yoga in the past. It has grown enormously in popularity over the past decade; in fact, over 300 million people practice yoga worldwide (Rakicevic, 2020). Yoga poses can be used standalone or integrated into mixed exercise routines in order to focus on flexibility, core strength, and balance. Many people practice yoga for physical health benefits without necessarily incorporating spirituality into the workout. This is an entirely valid way to participate in yogic exercise, and still provides holistic health benefits.

Even the most agnostic forms of yoga are holistic in nature, due to the multi-faceted nature of the activity. Yogic poses target your physical body, while also focusing on mindfulness, focus, relaxation, and other mental/spiritual benefits. According to a 2012 survey, over 94% of yogis said they used it to enhance their personal wellness. Those surveyed said that they practiced yoga to treat stress, lack of sleep, and emotional unrest, in addition to keeping fit (Rakicevic, 2020).

Structured yoga practice also tends to focus on keeping a holistically healthy lifestyle outside of your routine, in order to bring your best self to the mat every day. Studies show that yoga students tend to lead healthier lifestyles over all, and over 40% say they eat healthier food because of their practice (Rakicevic, 2020). Much like other traditional medicine techniques, yoga is focused on every aspect of your personal health, not just your physical fitness.

This is why many people eventually find themselves attached to the more spiritual elements of the practice. Yoga is over 5000 years old (Rakicevic, 2020), and has been used in tandem with religion and spiritual medicine since its origins. Those who dive deeper into the dogma of yogic teachings will find that spiritual alignment and self-discipline are core principles of the art. True yogis invest in the health of their chakras, balanced energy, and mindful awareness of their lifestyle choices.

While there is more than one way to practice yoga in the modern era, the more holistic aspects hold root within tradition. To better understand how I could use yoga to strengthen my spiritual bodywork, I took time to learn about the ancient yoga sutras.

Yoga Sutras and the Eight Limbs

Over 2000 years ago, an Indian scholar by the name of Patanjali wrote a four-chapter piece entitled *Yoga Sutras*. These outlined 196 sutras, each outlining a core tenet of proper yoga practice, and their meaning in a broader spiritual philosophy. Sutra comes from the same linguistic root as the word suture, which means "to connect" or "hold together" (Gabriel, 2018). This emphasizes the theme of wholeness behind each of the yoga sutras and the broader theory behind yoga in general. These are 196 different guiding values to make your yogic practice meaningful and healing.

One of the topics discussed in these sutras is human suffering. Patanjali indicates a few causes of anguish that are commonly held by those who suffer too much in life. Some of these include living egotistically and forgetting your identity (Gabriel, 2018), which are both core elements acknowledged through spiritual healing. By focusing too much on your pride, or neglecting the self, you are diminishing the power of your spirit. Over time, this can lead to chronic pain, emotional turmoil, or other forms of suffering. By acknowledging these in the sutras, yoga aims to lead you away from these bad habits.

Another teaching the sutra provides is about the true nature of stress and wellness. The yoga sutras emphasize that stress is a major blocker for inner peace and balance in your life. Too much stress can eventually lead to exhaustion, which will eventually lead to a lack of energy and motivation. This, in turn, brings lethargy and eventually mental unwellness (Gabriel, 2018). Eventually, this leads to factors that cause more stress in your life. From there, you may suffer from repeated emotional problems, physical disorders, or spiritual blockages as the cycle continues.

The solution to this that the sutras suggest comes from the practice of self-discipline. This is a key element to spiritual yoga, and drives your healing process by teaching you better habits. By being committed to your yoga routine, you are learning to show up, keep yourself accountable, and push through difficult tasks for the betterment of yourself. The structure of yogic dogma projects these elements onto the routine itself, and shows you how to bring them into your daily life as well.

This is best explained through the eight limbs of yoga. This is a concept introduced within Patanjali's *Yoga Sutra* and is still taught by traditional yogis today. These limbs are eight major observances that represent the core elements of yogic teachings (Gabriel, 2018). By following these guidelines, you can turn any set of yoga poses that you enjoy into a more wholesome, traditional exercise.

There are a few different ways to interpret and implement each of these ideas, but they can be summarized for common use in your spiritual healing practice.

Yama	Practice nonviolence, honesty, generosity, and respect towards others. Do not steal, waste, or become greedy.
Niyama	Live your life with firm principles of

	purity, studiousness, devotion, and spirituality.
Asana	Move your body with consciousness and intent. This limb is where the poses and physical practice comes into play. Most casual yogis focus primarily on asana.
Pranayama	Use spiritual breathing exercises to energize and expand your life force.
Pratyahara	Practice introspection and turn inwards to examine the self.
Dharana	Train your mind to meditate and sharpen your sense of concentration. Control your ability to harness and maintain attention on a singular task or idea.
Dhyana	Continuous, perfected meditation, focused on energetic flow and spiritual acceptance.
Samadhi	Find unity and become one with your spirit, the universe, and the divine.

Information used in this chart is sourced from Roger Gabriel's article *Yoga Sutras 101: Everything You Need to Know,* written for Chopra (Gabriel 2019).

These limbs each represent an aspect of mindfulness and traditional dogma that you can incorporate into your yoga practice for a more spiritually fulfilling experience. You may have noticed that many of these ideas line up with fundamentals of other exercises outlined in this guide, or from your own personal experience with holistics. This is no coincidence.

As one of the oldest forms of spiritual bodywork, yoga operates on the same foundational building blocks that are used in adjacent techniques. You can use these sutras alongside your yoga poses or as guiding principles of your meditation, visualization, or other healing exercises.

Breathwork

One of my favorite types of spiritual medicine is holistic breathwork. This comes in many forms, but even the most basic spiritual breathing techniques can provide new perspectives to your healing journey.

Those who regularly practice breathwork as part of their holistic routine find that it's one of the best ways to channel energy through the body, reaping great mental and emotional health benefits. By using your natural ability to breathe, you can learn the impact of awareness training and synchronizing your air flow with your spiritual self. People frequently use breathwork to treat emotional pain, reduce stress, boost the immune system, improve social relationships, inspire creativity, and cleanse negative thoughts (Cronkleton, 2019), just to name a few examples. This comes from concentrated exercises where you intentionally alter your breathing in order to change the chemistry of your body, and pair it with meditative mantras or thought exercises to enhance your inner synchronicity.

There are a few categories of basic frameworks you can use to structure different breathing exercises. This section will focus on breathwork you can do alone at home. If you're interested in more advanced techniques, you can see a professional naturopath who holds holotropic or rebirthing breathing sessions. These are intense exercises designed to limit the amount of oxygen taken in at once, and send you into an altered state of consciousness. Individuals experienced in these techniques claim that it can have a profound effect on your spiritual energy, and provide enlightening epiphanies about the state of your inner self (Cronkleton, 2019). I highly recommend seeing a practitioner for one of these sessions if you're interested, but since the effects can be physically and emotionally extreme, you should not attempt to perform them alone.

For your home practice, there are a few essential exercises you can learn in order to incorporate them into your spiritual bodywork routines. These are fundamental exercises that teach you how to set intention into your breathing, and how to pay attention to the way your breath makes you feel, physically, emotionally, and energetically. Consider these methods as tried and true sketches that you can memorize and color over in more detail once you understand their shape.

When you find that one or more of these types of breathwork has an effect on you, embrace it. Repeat it and reinforce it in a dedicated session on a regular schedule. By setting aside time and making a commitment to show up, you are imbuing your healing practice with significance. This has a potent effect on your process, and makes it more powerful in the long run.

After you've done these basics time and time again, and learned when you need them most, you can add them to other spiritual medicine techniques that you enjoy. Breathwork can be easily incorporated into acupressure sessions, yoga routines, meditations, visualizations, and Reiki healing exercises.

Diaphragm Breathwork

This type of breathing exercise focuses on activating your diaphragm and using it to power deeper inhalation and exhalation. It can also be referred to as belly breathing and is the most common type of breathing used in conjunction with meditation (Jewell, 2018).

Steps:

1. Find a comfortable seat or place to lie down. You should be at ease, and require minimal effort to sustain the position over a period of time.
2. Begin to take full, casual breaths, letting yourself fall into a natural rhythm.
3. Bring your attention to your neck and shoulders, and let them relax. Breathe like this for a few moments, and check in with your shoulders again. Relax them again, if need be.

4. Gently place one hand on your stomach, and the other on your chest. Let them rest there without pressure, and feel yourself breathe.
5. Slowly change your breathing so that you inhale through your nose, and purse your lips to exhale, like you're blowing through a straw.
6. Like this, take a deep breath inwards for two seconds. Feel it travel through your nose, down into your stomach.
7. Exhale for two seconds through your pursed mouth, letting your belly sink through the breath.
8. Allow yourself to experience the way your belly expands and lifts, and then release the thought along with your exhale. Your stomach should rise and sink significantly with your breath, while your chest remains relatively still.
9. Repeat this for as long as you feel comfortable. If you want, you can set a timer for 5-20 minutes for this exercise, or just let yourself experience it without a time limit.

(Jewell, 2018)

Box Breathing

This is one of the simplest breathwork techniques I've used in my work as a healer. It's highly effective for increasing concentration and inducing a relaxed state (Gotter, 2017). You can use box breathing during dedicated healing sessions, or while at work, social events, and other stressful situations out and about.

Steps:

1. Find a comfortable position, whether seated, lying down, or otherwise relaxed.
2. Get into a natural rhythm of relaxing, intentional breaths. Once you feel ready, you can begin this exercise with a slow, conscious exhale.
3. Inhale through your nose, and slowly count to four. Allow yourself to feel the breath in your lungs, and visualize them filling up, section by section, until your chest is full of warm air.
4. Hold your breath and count to four again. You should feel content here, not strained.
5. Exhale slowly through your mouth, counting to four. Imagine the breath gently releasing from your lungs and spreading out into the air around you.
6. Repeat this for as long as you feel comfortable. You can do this for long sessions for the full experience, or a few cycles of breath if you just need a moment to calm down.

(Gotter, 2017)

4-7-8 Technique

This technique is very similar to box breathing, if not a successor to it. You'll follow the same basic steps as the prior exercise, but use a count of 4-7-8 instead of 4-4-4. Many people use this form of breathwork to fall asleep, or to induce a deeper state of relaxation (Gotter, 2018).

Steps:

1. Begin your breathwork in an isolated location, sitting comfortably, or lying in a relaxed position.
2. Release any breath you're holding with a big exhale, blowing it through your lips.
3. Inhale through your nose, focusing only on the sensation of the breath, and count to four in your head.
4. After four counts, hold your breath, and count to seven. During this time, try to center your thoughts on the counting. If your thoughts begin to wander, gently guide them back to this.
5. Exhale for eight counts, blowing the air through your lips again. Let yourself indulge in this release, and enjoy the long breath.
6. Repeat for as long as you feel comfortable.

(Gotter, 2018)

New Experiences Nourish the Body

There are countless examples of bodywork techniques that I was not able to cover in this chapter. I hope that this sample of exercises has piqued your curiosity, as I invite you to experiment and listen to what your body tells you about them. Try things that appeal to you, or put your own spin on them if you want to spice things up. If you're interested in more advanced versions of acupressure, yoga, or breathwork, I highly recommend reading about other people's healing experiences. There is no better way to learn what works for you than to see what works for others.

By venturing out and indulging that curiosity, you are engaging in the most fundamental aspect of spiritual bodywork. Integrating fitness training, healthy eating, and other physical treatments into your life in a holistic way allows you to find that connection between your body, mind, and spirit. Allowing your emotions, motivations, beliefs, and experiences to influence the way you think about your physical vessel is vital to its health. Your body is a living, breathing part of you, and it deserves to have regular conversations with you. If you give it the same old treatment every day, you aren't allowing it to grow and thrive along with the rest of your beautiful self.

Open up to new things, and expand your horizons. Be a little daring sometimes, or let yourself relax if you find that your life is always moving too quickly. Above all else, listen to what your body is telling you. Aches and pains mean something, and that something is not always going to be obvious. Get in touch with your body's spiritual language, and let it fuel your healing practice.

Do a little better each day, bring commitment to your sessions, and cherish the energy your body provides. Whether you're strengthening your body, or using your body to strengthen the rest of you, that power is yours to own. Embrace it. Brag about it. Make sure that you really feel it.

Chapter 4:

Channeling Through the Mind

Thoughts and feelings are the driving force behind much of human interaction. The way we view the world, as individuals, is inherently biased. Everything that we experience is filtered through our personal perception, and that's influenced by the way we think, above all else. This means that our minds directly control the information that gets processed, broken down, and eventually absorbed into the way we think of our lives.

That much may be obvious enough, but what does that mean for the health of your mental facilities? In the new, complex world we all live in, many things can influence the well-being of our minds. From 2017-2018, 19% of American adults identified that they experienced mental illness that significantly impacted their lives. Some of these common illnesses include depression, anxiety, and dissociation, and these numbers are only increasing in the past decade (MHA, 2012). Statistics like this are already startling, but they are still limited to those diagnosed with a psychological disorder.

Beyond the scope of illness itself, many people struggle with other symptoms of an unhealthy mind. Nervousness, anger, social isolation, lethargy, recklessness, and distraction are all common experiences that come from mental unwellness. A weakened mind can create issues with how you see the world, how you view yourself, and how you treat those things in the long run.

In many ways, the state of your thoughts directly influences the state of your life. Experiencing negative thoughts on a regular basis can prevent you from fulfilling your goals, keeping healthy habits, and reaching out for help when you need it. Your mind is the mouthpiece for your inner voice of reason, and when it's weakened, it might not be the voice you need.

For this same reason, your mind is also a vital source of healing for the rest of your body and spirit. If you're suffering from other problems, like chronic pain, or lack of purpose, you can use your mind as a powerful channel for healing energy. By learning to control your thoughts and feelings, you can use them to holistically affect the way you handle other problems in your life.

There's a good chance you already do this on some level in your mundane life. Have you ever been so cold that you imagine yourself on a sunny beach, soaking up the sun, just to distract yourself from the chilly environment? Maybe you've used a favorite snack or movie as a reward after a long day at work, making a hard day go by faster. These are little examples of how you can use the power of your mind to change the way your holistic self thrives in the world around you.

Within spiritual medicine, this theory is key to understanding the interconnectedness of the mind, body, and spirit. Many techniques used by holistic healers focus on using the mind as a channel for this potent energetic effect. This chapter will cover a few ways you can heal your mind with spiritual methods, and how to use your mind's energy to heal the body and spirit.

The Mind as a Tool

It doesn't take an expert spiritual healer to understand that the mind has control over almost everything we do. If our bodies are vessels with which we navigate the physical world, our minds are the navigators, making decisions and doing the legwork to make the body move how we want it to. When working in synchrony, our mental strength can give us the direction we need to make healthy decisions, keep our commitments, socialize with others, and otherwise make it possible for us to live fulfilling lives.

This doesn't mean we are always in control over our minds, though. As much as our thoughts and feelings can sometimes feel like the essence of us, it is only one element to the whole self. These mental functions give us the ability to process the world, and make conclusions based on those thoughts and feelings, but they are completely useless without a healthy body and spirit. Feeling happy and rational is great, but not if you are in so much pain that you can't get out of bed.

Conversely, being comfortable and fit only goes so far if you're saddled with stress and depression, and can't use your vitality to its fullest.

For me, it's easier to think of my mind as the primary tool that I can use to control my life. I'm not the boss of my thoughts, but they're not the boss of me either. Instead, I turn inward to examine my mind as an individual part of my whole. By opening myself up to dialog with my thoughts and feelings, I can understand where they're coming from, and learn to work with them instead of against them. Doing this allows you to figure out what your mind is capable of and use those capabilities to fill out your holistic healing toolbelt.

Western medical circles already acknowledge the ability humans have to use their mental tools to alter other aspects of their health. One example of this is the relationship between psoriasis and stress. Psoriasis is a medical condition that affects your auto-immune system, creates severe rashes, and causes inflammation and joint pain. Doctors have studied this condition and found that it can be commonly triggered and exacerbated by stress (Tanner Clinic, 2020). If you're experiencing an abundance of hardship in your life, or are prone to constant worrying, this mental anguish may provoke bodily conditions like psoriasis. The symptoms of these conditions tend to be painful, uncomfortable, and expensive, which can lead to more stress over time. This stress comes back around to make the problem even worse, or even leads to additional health problems on top of everything else.

Additionally, mental unwellness can change the way you seek out treatment, or maintain health in other parts of your life. In 2014, a study was done to determine if certain mental illnesses could affect longevity due to correlated health conditions. It found that these illnesses potentially reduce your life expectancy by up to 20 years. This margin is similar to the effect of heavy smoking (Tanner Clinic, 2020). This effect is not limited to psychological conditions, but is most noticeable when there is a diagnosis to highlight the problem at hand.

This is another reason spiritual medicine benefits from the holistic approach. By treating symptoms as part of your whole system, we can target the root of the problem and heal it with the help of your natural strong points. It's not always easy to attack mental ailments directly. Using spiritual thought and body synchronicity to influence the mind can be a helpful hand throughout the process.

The techniques I've chosen to include in this chapter cover a few different ways you can use your mind as a healing channel. They can be used to target mental ailments directly, or use mindfulness to address other symptoms in your life. Many of these methods can be used in conjunction with exercise, meditation, or hobbies you enjoy, so feel free to experiment with them as you get to understand how they work.

The main takeaway for most of these exercises is that you need to use your mind, not control it. Mental energy is some of the strongest power you hold as a spiritual being, and you will be surprised by the way it can impact your life. These techniques are designed to teach you how to be aware of your thoughts and feelings, and what you can gain from listening to them.

Sometimes a negative experience in your mind can seem too troublesome to deal with. Your instinct might be to shove trauma, sadness, or stress to the back of your head and ignore it. Spiritual medicine seeks to train you out of this. You should listen to those experiences and learn why they are happening. Your mind is thinking or feeling a certain way for a reason. Look deep, and try to understand it, instead of suppressing the knowledge provided to you.

Ignoring your mental health is like ignoring an expensive tool. You bought a fancy new thermometer for a reason. When it says it's 150 degrees outside, in the middle of winter, you should probably figure out why that's happening, instead of throwing the thing in the trash. If the thermometer is broken, you can fix it. If it's not, then you had better figure out what's happening outside.

Visualization and Affirmation

One of the fundamental ways that holistic healers harness the power of the mind is through creative visualization and positive affirmation. These are highly approachable techniques that anyone can try, without any supplies or specific training. Visualization is about harnessing the power of your imagination, and using it to train your mind, body, and spirit. Affirmation works in sync with this training, by reinforcing productive thought patterns.

For many people, finding the energy to make your goals a reality is tough. Sometimes, this can be due to a lack of motivation, a lack of focus, or a lack of belief in your own capabilities. Our minds are prone to getting stuck on ideas that may not be rational or useful to our personal desires. This can come from an inaccurate view of the self, and an inability to see a positive future for that version of you.

Visualization focuses on regular, focused sessions of setting goals, picturing them in your mind's eye, and letting yourself feel the result of seeing them completed. This may sound simple at first, but by doing this in a structured, repetitive process, the negative energy in your mind will begin to clear. Over time, your emotional and spiritual energy will be able to find those visualized thoughts, and make them feel more achievable (Bernstein, 2019). This can activate the motivation and initiative you need to manifest them into reality.

Affirmations can be used on their own, or in conjunction with this process. These are mantra-like reminders that you can use to reframe negative thoughts into more productive ones. A good affirmation comes as a result of introspection, and a strong relationship between you and your mind. By using visualization, meditation, and other introspective exercises, you can grow to understand the type of negative thoughts your mind is prone to latching onto. Once you recognize these problematic thoughts, you can stop them before they get a reaction out of you, and replace them with affirmations that you have trained on.

To use an example from my life, I like to think of my sister Katherine. Growing up, Katherine struggled with her weight, and was bullied in school for this. This kept her out of a lot of social groups, including sports teams and outdoor clubs. As a young adult, she came to believe that she just wasn't an athletic person, and wouldn't be able to keep up with an exercise routine. She suffered a lot from problems with her self-image and body shame, and for a long time she thought this was normal.

What ended up doing wonders for Kathy was attending a visualization meditation class. Her process began by doing focused exercises on a specific intention; she wanted to become more physically active. Her ultimate goal was to join an adult volleyball team at her work, but she didn't feel strong or confident enough to do so yet. During each visualization session, she begins the meditation by focusing on that intention. Then, she imagines a situation where the goal has already been met. For example, showing up at the volleyball club, wearing new work-out clothes, and being complimented by her coworkers. She concentrates on this image for the duration of the session, and ruminates on how it makes her feel.

By engaging with those feelings, she can train herself to be more accepting of a future where they are a reality. This is more than playing pretend, or having high hopes. It's about returning to this visualized ideal and concentrating on how it could look in your life.

You can also start using affirmations alongside other spiritual medicine practices to help eliminate negative thoughts that you have gotten used to. Whenever my sister found herself thinking things along the line of "I hate the way I look" or "I'm not strong enough to work out every day," she replaced those thoughts with positive affirmations. Then, she implemented those into her visualization exercises, to better associate those affirmations with the future she was trying to manifest. This trains your brain into thinking healthy thoughts, and having more faith in what you are capable of accomplishing.

This works through a process called manifestation. You can train your mind to visualize your goals, affirm them with positive statements, and come back to these ideas on a regular basis. In this way, you'll take your goals, and use your own natural mental energy to manifest them into reality (Bernstein, 2019). This not only makes it easier for you to transition into a better lifestyle, but empowers you to make that transition happen for yourself. Feeling in control over your future is a great motivator against negative thoughts.

Many problems rooted in an unhealthy mind can be accomplished were it not for symptoms of negativity. Self-esteem, body image, pessimism, and other symptoms of a negative outlook can make certain actions seem impossible to even the strongest individuals. By treating these thoughts directly, you can open up your mental channels for a healthier energetic flow and change these outlooks for yourself.

Visualization Exercises

The act of actualizing, creative, or meditative visualization can be done in many different contexts. Many people integrate this idea into everyday self-help exercises, or as an exercise in reframing their thoughts. Spiritual healers like to integrate visualization into meditation, yoga, massage, and other holistic practices. This is because this tool is designed to help you target your intent for a particular healing process, and facilitate your journey to the end of it.

For this section, I wanted to include instructions for a basic, standalone visualization exercise. You can do this on your own, with no preparation, as long as you can set aside 5-20 minutes in a private area for the session. These steps are designed to guide you through a visualization exercise on a particular intention or goal.

You can come to your session with almost any objective in mind. The best points of focus for visualization are things you can still learn about in your life. If you're struggling with depression, you might start off with a goal of self-discovery. Take time to ruminate on situations where you've noticed your depression in the past. Think about how this affects your life, and what the consequences are. Maybe this depression keeps you from socializing, or taking care of your body the right way.

Once you've spent time introspecting on these issues, imagine what it would look like if these problems went away. Picture a life after your healing is completed, where you have more energy, healthier relationships, and a cleaner home. Even if it doesn't seem possible, take time during your visualization practice to detail this future and memorize the shape of it. Embrace how it makes you feel.

After you've done this a few times, you can deepen your practice by opening your mind to those feelings. While picturing this future, you can ask it what steps are taken to get there. When in a relaxed, meditative state, you may find that answers come to you naturally. You may also find that you don't know, and that's okay too. These sessions should be dedicated to making that picture of the future, revisiting it, and reframing your beliefs about how possible it really is (Bernstein, 2019).

This is a simple, beginner's framework for this type of visualization exercise. If you want to try it out, make sure you spend time on it before making decisions about the practice. You should set a specific time in your schedule committed to these sessions, and hold yourself accountable to show up. This is part of the process. If you find that this exercise provides insight to you, or has a meaningful affect in your life, feel free to add more to it. Use it while practicing yoga, or taking a walk, or using crystal healing, if it feels right. The best part about spiritual visualization is that the entire process belongs to you, so make it yours!

In Chapter 6, there are a few guided meditations that include visualization and affirmation during the exercise. These might be appealing if you're looking for an example of how to integrate these techniques into your healing regime.

Steps:

1. Begin your session in a private area that you feel a strong attachment to. This could be your bedroom, living room, or somewhere outdoors. The important part is that you feel ownership and comfort in this place.

2. Find a comfortable seat, or lie down. Your body should be at ease, so you require no tension to keep it in this position.
3. Start your session with an empowering affirmation that is meaningful to you. This can be something as simple as "I believe that I have control over my future" or "I am a powerful, spiritual woman." You can also use something more specific to your life. If you need suggestions, see the next section for some possibilities.
4. Begin visualizing. Imagine the future you want to manifest.
5. Start off with what it looks like. Think of all the details that would exist in this future. What are you wearing? Who do you see with you? How do you get there, and when do you leave?
6. Add more depth to the visualization by inviting other senses. Maybe you imagine the smell of the room, or the texture of the floor beneath you. What's the temperature in this scenario? What kind of sounds do you hear?
7. Focus on this visualization for as long as you feel comfortable in it. You can set a timer for 5-20 minutes, or let the session last for as long as you like.
8. If your mind begins to wander, let it do so for a few moments. Take note of what you think, and the associations your mind is making to the visualization. What does it say about your

feelings on this future? Is it negative, or positive? Does it help, or hurt?

9. After acknowledging the thought, gently guide yourself back to the visualization. Go through each of the details again until your concentration stays on the picture.

10. When your session is over, bring yourself back to reality, and take time to reflect. You may benefit from writing your thoughts down in a journal, or printing pictures that represent what you visualized. These methods will allow you to revisit this later, and invite new conclusions from the information.

When reflecting on this exercise, ask yourself a few questions. If you found yourself thinking negative thoughts during the session, find a positive affirmation that pushes back. Use them during your next sessions, or in response to those thoughts in the future.

Even if it seems silly, continue returning to your practice with the intent of making your hopes a reality. Over time, it will become easier to believe in that intent. Eventually, your belief will drive you to confidently pursue your goals and manifest that future you created for yourself.

Affirmations

Using affirmations in your healing practice is a great way to combat naturally occurring negative thoughts that crop up against your will. Everyone has that nagging voice in their head that speaks up when the mind is at its weakest. This is common, but it isn't a healthy habit to fall into. These intrusive thoughts tend to reflect insecurities or stressors going on in our lives. They can be indicators that something deeper is wrong, and for that they're useful. Experiencing an abundance of negative thoughts can be a sign that you need to address an underlying issue in your mind, body, or spirit. That doesn't mean you shouldn't strive to combat those thoughts, though.

Affirmations serve to be direct opposition to negative thoughts. They are designed to be said out loud, and reiterated in mental exercises. By repeating these simple mantras, you remind yourself of your core beliefs, and unhealthy thoughts tend to hold a little less weight.

Have you ever been in a bad mood, and found yourself jumping to conclusions about everyone around you? Then, after you feel better, those conclusions seem absolutely ridiculous? Affirmations target that exact cycle, but aim to nip the negative thoughts in the bud before they can fester and cause you mental unrest. By learning the traps your mind falls into, you can prepare for them, and use practiced affirmations to remind yourself what you really believe.

"I am enough."	"I believe I can do better."
"I can't be held responsible for other people's decisions."	"I know what is best for my body."

"People enjoy my presence."	"My decisions are my own to make."
"I am worth more than that."	"No one else can limit what I'm capable of."
"It's okay to root for myself."	"I know myself better than anyone else."
"The world will not end if I make a mistake."	"I am not afraid of the unknown."
"Others are not in charge of how I feel."	"I believe I am worthy of love."
"It's okay to reward myself for doing something good."	"No one else can see things the way I do."
"Failing just means my ambitions are high."	"I am the only one that can stop me from achieving my dreams."

Above, I've included some of my favorite affirmations for various circumstances. These are intended to be suggestions, inspiration, or examples for you to use, so don't be too hung up on finding one that fits your exact situation. You can use these to start with, or come up with your own affirmations that resonate with your beliefs.

Aromatherapy

A lot of sensations can stimulate healing energy in different parts of your system. Scent is one of the most powerful abilities that humans possess. Our sense of smell is directly tied to memory, and can be used to make potent emotional associations with certain fragrances.

Spiritual medicine uses aromatherapy to harness this natural ability, and tie it to the holistic, whole-self experience. By using scented substances, most often in the form of essential oils or incense, you can manipulate the emotional energy charged within any environment. This kind of therapy is almost always used in conjunction with other holistic treatments, but can be highly beneficial on its own. Applying essential oils to your clothes, body, bath, or other significant components of your everyday life can draw your mind to specific associations made with them, and allow you to anchor to those feelings.

People have been using essential oils for aromatherapy for over 6000 years (Brazier, 2017) This ancient practice has been a key part of spiritual medicine throughout its development over the centuries. Aromatherapy oils can be used to aid in holistic massage, meditation, breathwork, and any other practice that benefits from having control over your state of mind. The influence that fragrance has over our mental state is easily used for physical and spiritual benefits as well, making it a great tool for holistic practitioners.

Most people use essential oils through inhalation. This is the typical method people think of when they imagine aromatherapy. The fragrant oils are usually filtered through a diffuser, spray, steam, or other atomizer in order to spread the particles around in the air. Then, while your natural breath takes them in, the fragrance particles will begin to interact with your body, mind, and overall energetic flow.

This begins in your brain, as the essential oil molecules are absorbed by your limbic system. This is the part of your brain that processes memory and emotions; coincidentally, it's also the part that interacts with smell. Your olfactory gland exists within this structure, and works alongside it to handle all of these different factors. The limbic system monitors the chemicals and hormones that control the way you process emotions, and distributes them around the body. In this way, it also affects your heart rate, breathing, blood pressure, and other physical parts of your body, based on the emotion related chemicals it produces (Brazier, 2017).

Understanding this fundamental medical aspect of your brain is the first step to explaining how aromatherapy really works. Some people think that having good smells around simply calms you down because they're pleasant to experience. Obviously, it is not that simple. Different types of smells produce different chemical reactions within your limbic system, causing varied emotional and physical responses. Because of this process, you can use aromatherapy to influence these responses, and control how you feel.

Aromatherapy is commonly used for a wide variety of ailments. This works because essential oils (and other aromatherapeutic products) come in many different fragrances, all of which have different effects on the human mind, body, and spirit. Some of the proven holistic health benefits of aromatherapy include treatment for nausea, headaches, body aches, anxiety, stress, depression, insomnia, fatigue, menstrual symptoms, menopausal symptoms, and hair loss (Brazier, 2017).

Many people also find essential oils useful for aiding in concentration during spiritual exercises. This works by providing a calming energy in the environment you are healing in, while also maintaining a distinctive, noticeable smell in the room. When entering a deeper state of consciousness, or a repetitive meditation, having a strong fragrance can be an unobtrusive way of centering your focus on something external. This can keep your mind from wandering away from its intended task, and remind you of your purpose when you find the familiar scent. This makes aromatherapy an excellent complementary treatment for any holistic healing practice.

Most practitioners of aromatherapy, professional and casual, use essential oils as their preferred medium. This is because they are highly concentrated, sourced from natural materials, and easy to infuse in multiple ways. You can diffuse oils into a room, or apply them topically, if you prefer them to be directly on your skin.

If you choose a topical method of aromatherapy oils, make sure you understand the potency of the oil, and the recommended dosage. While a strong smell won't kill you, too much fragrant oil can cause skin irritation and even painful damage if applied incorrectly. The oil you receive should have its recommended dosage listed on the bottle (Brazier, 2017). If you're unsure, consult a naturopath or medical doctor about whether or not your skin might have an adverse reaction to topical essential oils.

In addition, you should be aware of the differences between purely aromatherapeutic oils and aromatherapy massage oils. These come from the same essential scents, but the chemistry of the oil is different. Oils used for massage are usually mixed with a diluting oil acting as a carrier (Brazier, 2017). This makes it less harsh on your skin, and more soothing for the massage, while still bringing the fragrance into the experience. Don't apply the same amount of essential oil to your skin as you would with massage oil, or you may experience an overdose that causes an adverse skin reaction.

Otherwise, there is no reason to choose diffusion or topical application, other than personal preference. Some essential oils come in individual rollers that you can apply like perfume, letting you receive aromatherapeutic benefits while out and about in your daily routine. Since almost all of these oils smell nice, most people won't even notice you're wearing something for a medical purpose. This can be a great way to reduce chronic anxiety or headaches in the workplace or social gatherings.

In the chart below, I've included some of the most popular (and my most favorite) aromatherapy fragrances and their healing effects. These are all sourced from natural ingredients, a.k.a. smells made from mother earth.

Please be aware of any potential allergies you might have to these oils, as well. Some of these natural ingredients can induce allergic reactions in people who are sensitive to those substances. If you have allergies, or experience symptoms after using an essential oil, ask your doctor before continuing the treatment.

While I've included the most common experiences people have with these particular scents, feel free to try some out just because you think they smell good. A certain essential oil may have a unique effect for you depending on your relationship with that scent, and emotional memories you associate with it. Aromatherapy is about body chemistry and mental association, so everyone's experience is a little different. If you have a fond memory of a loved one that always drank Earl Grey tea, bergamot might bring you more relaxation than it would for others. This is one of the benefits of using personalized, holistic medicine.

Aromatherapeutic Fragrances

Chamomile	Treats skin irritation, eczema, and reduces stress.
Eucalyptus	Opens the respiratory system, and treats congestion, cough, and other cold/flu symptoms.
Jasmine	Increases libido, stimulation, and alertness; excites energy levels and influences blood flow

Lavender	Reduces stress, relieves headaches, and treats symptoms of insomnia
Peppermint	Treats nausea and stomach aches, can relieve tightness in the chest
Lemon	Boosts happiness, energy levels, and comfort; reduces symptoms of depression
Sandalwood	Increases energy levels, stimulation, and libido
Rosemary	Treats hair loss and muscle spasms; improves memory retention
Pepper	Stimulates blood flow and circulation; soothes muscle pain and tension
Lemongrass/Citronella	Acts as a natural mosquito repellent, reduces stress
Tea	Treats acne, irritated skin, and bug bites.
Yarrow	Soothes inflammation of the joints, relieves symptoms of

	the cold/flu

The information in this chart was retrieved from Yvette Brazier's article *Aromatherapy: What You Need to Know,* written for Medical News Today (Brazier, 2017).

Nurturing the Mind with Acceptance

The greatest thing you can do for the health of your mind is to embrace the strengths and weaknesses it naturally holds. No human brain is the same, and there is no such thing as a "perfect" person. Your mind is going to have its little quirks and oddities to it, and some of them are fine to indulge in. What you need to remember is that even the worst things your thoughts will put you through are still worth paying attention to.

When using spiritual medicine, you should always find yourself open and ready to accept anything that comes at you during the practice. When using visualization exercises or aromatherapy in your healing session, make sure you take a moment to really experience what you are feeling in those moments. Your emotions are just as much a part of your mind as your thoughts are, and they speak a different language.

Even when you identify that something in your mental process is "off," or fueled by negative energy, take a moment to offer acceptance to that moment. Take in the thought, and accept that it's a part of you. You don't need to eliminate everything that influenced that thought or brought it into being. Instead, you should find what caused it to form into such a negative form, and see how you can heal that root cause.

Taking time to embrace even these negative thoughts and emotions can ultimately teach you not to dwell on them in the future. Even the worst feeling in the entire world will come and go, and eventually be ancient history. By acknowledging that it exists, you can start the process of treating it and making your mind a better place to be in the future.

Chapter 5:

Channeling Through the Spirit

Of the mind, body, and spirit, the latter is often the most complex to explain to newcomers in this field. Spiritual medicine focuses on the spirit as the fundamental healing force present in every human being. When a practice focuses on the mind or body, it's pretty straight-forward how that process affects the overall health of the whole. The spirit is an equally important element to confront, but it is largely invisible, and the most abstract part of our holistic health.

We've already discussed the various interpretations of the spirit in Chapter 2, but what does that mean for healing? Through some of the methods already outlined in this guide, you've learned to channel spiritual energy through your mind and body. This energy is strong, and if you've experienced it already, you may sense that there's more that it can do for you.

Getting to understand the nature of your spiritual energy is the first step to using it as a medium for growth. Some holistic techniques target areas of your mind and body to affect the flow of energy indirectly. Others, like the ones I've selected to feature in this chapter, confront the energy directly, in order to wake up the connections to the mind and body.

Using the spirit as a channel is an inherently non-invasive healing process. Spiritual medicine techniques focus on utilizing your own inherent energy as the primary avenue for self-improvement. Humans are highly powerful energetic beings. Your spiritual channel can boost your immune system and spark the innate ability of your body to fight off disease and negative influences (Mason, 2010). This is only one example of the strength that spiritual energy has to invigorate the health of the whole self.

Many people use their spiritual energy channels to set intention, and manifest that intention as a tangible, healing force. This can do wonders for the health of the self, by sparking motivation, changing perspective, and imbuing purpose into the everyday acts of life.

A common misconception about using spirituality for this purpose is that this is similar to "faith healing." Faith healers are often criticized for implying that prayer, or other religious acts, are all you need in order to overcome discomfort. This is not the perspective that spiritual medicine takes, even in the slightest (Mason, 2010).

Spiritual healing is grounded in reality, as a core principle. The fundamental natural power that humans hold is the driving force behind this practice. We want to focus on your real, tangible experiences. The feelings, thoughts, sensations, pains, and beliefs that you live with are significant parts of your life. By denying these parts of yourself, you are suppressing this version of the world as you know it. That isn't good for your health, and those effects are very real.

This essential power that humans hold is both a boon and a challenge. While your innate healing energy is an important resource for you to harness, it can also create a sort of inertia to overcome (Mason, 2010).

Because your essence is strong, it can get stuck in its ways. When your spiritual channels are healthy, and your energy flows, this is a good thing. It can create a robust resistance to negative forces, and defend you against toxic influences. That being said, when you have a weaker spirit, or your energy is weak, this can become a habit within your overall system. Just like your mind and body, your spirit can get used to bad conditions, and become stunted as a result.

Then, that natural inertia that it holds becomes a wall between you and your healing. When you confront the spirit, you are engaging with it in the same way you might engage with your mind and body. You must open yourself up to the spirit and create a dialog, converse with your energy, and understand its needs. This is the first step to breaking through that momentum, and finding out what pushes it in the wrong direction.

The exercises in this chapter are designed to connect you with your spiritual channels and fully experience the energy flowing through them. This comes with a few expectations from you, during the process.

You must enter spiritual healing with a dedication to introspection, mindfulness, and openness. By following these three principles at the core of your practice, you can come back to them when you hit that wall of inertia. When you meet resistance from your spirit, or feel that you are making no progress, you must remind yourself that this process is about more than just the end result. It is a journey, and how you treat yourself during this journey is the most important part of it.

Revisiting the Spirit

Learning controlled dedication is the first step towards self-discipline. A key part of spiritual medicine is teaching yourself to reflect, and lead your life with intention. This is why many holistic practices focus on concentration, commitment, and centering. A healthy spirit holds these traits with confidence, and uses them to understand their self before acting upon it.

During your healing journey, you may find yourself focused on the end goal. Resist this urge, and focus on the path you're currently traveling. Learning to use your spiritual energy correctly first requires you to unlearn the toxic expectations you hold for it already. These techniques are designed to remind you that your spirit is present and alive, and teach you to check in with it when you feel lost.

Going back to our metaphor of the ship. We've already covered the vessel and the crew of the boat that represents you; but what about the rest? The best captain on the best ship is only as useful as their destination. Your spirit represents the map, the route, and the stars that guide its trip across those choppy waters. This is the energy that brings the boat out onto the ocean in the first place, and motivates the crew to get where they're going.

Without healthy spiritual energy flowing through your channels, you may find yourself feeling purposeless. This is why recognizing your spirit is important. The acknowledgment you give to that energy is what enables your mind and body to find their holistic connection to it. If you have a map on board, but your crew won't read it, what use is it? It can be easy to ignore our spiritual health, simply because it is not as visible to us as our mental and physical conditions may be. Spiritual medicine has been developed over centuries to fight back against those tendencies and force you to acknowledge that part of you that you may be neglecting.

The spiritual perspective hinges upon the theory that everything in our universe is connected. This world is made up of vast, interwoven systems of energy, forming a cycle throughout the people, animals, and objects that inhabit it. Our energy is a part of this system, and it can be manipulated through an understanding of these systems.

This understanding comes with repetitive practice and mindful training of the mind, body, and spirit. Finding unity within one's self is a process, and it requires that you make the decision to complete that process.

Individuals who find a connection to their spiritual energy are able to use their own channels to heal themselves, and with enough practice, to heal others. This comes from that core concept of the energetic channels, and the spiritual connection between beings. With practice, you can learn what spiritual energy feels like, and how to determine the nature of that energy.

Once you're familiar with it, you can influence these flows by stimulating the natural currents within the spiritual channels. This can come through touch, sound, vibrations, or meditation, as just a few examples. The spirit isn't like blood or flesh; you can't simply remove the bad energy and replace it with fresh, clean stuff. Healthy energy comes from within, which means that you can heal it by waking up those innate processes that your body already knows how to do.

Reiki

By getting in touch with your channels, you can also learn to direct that energy to specific locations in your own body, or others. This is the foundation of Reiki energy healing.

This technique works through the laying of hands onto different energetic focal points around the body. It is an ancient practice that targets your innate life force, clearing blockages within it, and revitalizing it into a healthy state. The hands are used as a vector to transfer energy from the healer's palms, into the focal points of the patient.

Reiki can be done to balance the positive and negative forces within your spirit, cleanse blockages with an influx of new energy, or remove problematic energies from your system. Hands hold a high concentration of intersection points, making it a hub for active energy (Newman, 2017). This fact is also seen through the use of acupressure, since many effective pressure points are located in the palms, fingers, and wrists.

Think of it like a highway turnpike in a busy city. Traffic is guided throughout the city in metered, measured paths, in order to prevent huge jams in popular areas. Because of this, most streets in neighborhoods or marketplaces are pretty easy to navigate. Eventually, that traffic needs to be directed to a faster system of roads in order to keep those smaller streets free. This is where highways come into play, allowing faster speeds and more cars to travel on one set of roads. These roads tend to crossover in certain places, making these turnpikes the point where many cars ultimately get in and out of the city.

Similarly, energy can move all around your body, and be released from different points along the way. Your hands serve as a turnpike in the system, with several different paths intersecting through your palms. This means that as you learn to control when energy is released and absorbed, your hands become powerful healing tools.

Reiki is commonly performed by professional naturopaths in clinical settings. This is because many aspects of the practice are easily done with the aid of a practitioner, making it easy to pair with massage, acupressure, or other treatments. Having someone else to perform the treatment on you makes it a relaxing, hands-off experience, which can highlight certain aspects of the experience.

That being said, there are several ways that you can implement the art of Reiki healing on your own terms. Self-administered energy healing offers just as many benefits as seeing a professional, while being more approachable to those who want to incorporate it into their practice at home.

The fundamentals of Reiki are easy to learn, and take practice to master. Everything comes down to your connection with the energy, and using hand positions passed down from traditional Reiki healers. These positions are designed to maximize the connective points between your palms and the intersections of energy channels around your body (Newman, 2017).

One important thing to remember when guiding your own practice is that relaxation is part of the process. If you're taking charge of your own Reiki healing, then it can't become a source of stress for you along the way. You should always create a calming environment for your Reiki healing to take place. Essential oils, energetic crystals, and ambient music may be good additions to your session. These not only provide a soothing environment, but create conscious anchors to hold onto during the practice.

As you experience the transfer of energy during a Reiki session, you might experience intense emotions or sensations. These can be distracting, or even overwhelming during the process (Newman, 2017). By having a familiar anchor in your environment, you can reach out to that fragrance, crystal, or sound during the session, and bring yourself back to a place of center.

You should also remember that nothing about this practice needs to be perfect. Reiki hand positions are designed to work in synchrony with your inner rhythms, and you should always follow what feels right. If your hand positions are a little off, or you find yourself forgetting details, don't think of this as a failure. The practice will still be successful, and you'll become more precise over time.

Self-Driven Reiki Exercise

On average, each Reiki session can last anywhere from 20-90 minutes (Cleveland Clinic, 2019). This length is honestly up to you, and the time for which you feel you receive the most benefit from the exercise. Since you're running the show, you have more freedom to engage with shorter sessions. If you want to do a quick, 10-minute Reiki exercise after a long day at work, nothing is stopping you from dipping your toes in. By self-administering this type of healing energy, you don't have to worry about making an appointment that is too long, too short, or too expensive for what you get out of it.

The exercise I've outlined in this section is a straight-forward, basic Reiki healing session. I wanted to show you what it looks like to go through a series of different hand positions, stand-alone, without the aid of a practitioner or additional therapy. You may find that certain positions do more for you than others. This has to do with the specific needs of your spiritual energy.

When you first start experimenting with self-guided Reiki, I recommend going through all of the hand positions, even if some of them don't feel "necessary" for your current state. You may find that with repetition, you're gaining unexpected benefits from clearing these channels (Cleveland Clinic, 2019). If not, you're still practicing concentration, commitment, and control by completing the entire routine, and that's valuable to your spiritual health.

If you're doing a 20-minute Reiki session, you should use each of these positions for around 2 minutes. This means that for a 40 minute session, you should do 4 minutes in each hand position. For a longer session, like 90 minutes, you may want to limit each position to 4-6 minutes, and then do a second round, rather than spend 9 minutes on each step at once (Cleveland Clinic, 2019).

Either way, don't focus too much on timing. These are guidelines to give you a feel for the amount of time the energy needs to be concentrated to be effective, but you should always follow your spirit. Everyone is different, and you may find that a certain area needs more time than the rest of your body. Trust this instinct, and trust what your energy is telling you. Counting minute by minute does not foster a relaxing environment for you, and may alter your energetic state during the healing. This will give you a bad perspective on your current energy levels.

For this exercise, I've written the steps for a 30-minute session. This is one you can fit into a lunch break, a morning routine, or right before bed. If you want to lengthen the session, feel free to do so by sustaining your hands in these areas for longer, or doing a second rotation. This treatment will target the overall health of your energy. It aims to induce relaxation, reduce stress, clear negative blockages, and restore your natural energetic flow.

Steps:

1. Find a comfortable seat, in a chair, on a bed, or on the floor. You should be sitting upright, so that you have access to your upper body and legs.
2. Begin by placing your palms together, gently pressing your hands against each other. You can hold them like this against your chest, or right beneath your chin. Hold this position for around 3 minutes, taking deep, natural breaths.
3. Focus on your breathing during this position. Let yourself fall into an even rhythm, and let yourself concentrate on how your breath feels in your body.
4. Visualize the inhale and exhale as a cycle throughout your body. As you do this, reflect on the way it alters your energy levels. Do you feel balanced? Do you feel calm, or stimulated? Does any part of you feel different than the rest?
5. Move your hands gently to the top of your head. Let gravity naturally press your palms down into the surface of your scalp, and focus on that feeling for around 3 minutes.
6. Continue your even breaths throughout this position. If it feels right, you can add soft,

pressured movements to your palms, to massage your scalp.

7. Move your palms down to cover your eyes. Your hands should rest over your face, without restricting your breathing, for around 3 minutes. Bring your attention to the muscles in your forehead, cheeks, and mouth. Let them relax.
8. Continue your even breaths, and let yourself feel where the energy flows. Do you feel tension leaving your muscles? How does the warmth in your hands travel across your face?
9. Move your right hand to your neck, and your left hand over your heart. Hold them here for around 3 minutes.
10. Feel the warmth coming from your throat, and the rhythm of your heartbeat. Take time to notice how this synchronizes with your natural breath cycle. Notice the way your body moves in unity with itself, and visualize how that looks within your spiritual channels.
11. Move your hands down again, underneath your breast line. Let your palms press gently against your stomach, and bring your middle fingers to connect at the center. Hold this position for 3 minutes.
12. Take note of your breathing. Make sure you return to a natural, even rhythm if you've strayed from it. Allow your hands to imbue your center with positive energy, and relax the muscles of your chest and back.

13. Move your hands down, in a straight line, to rest below the navel. Experience the way your natural warmth travels down with them.
14. Hold them here for another 3 minutes, continuing to concentrate on the tension in your torso, and the rhythm of your breathing.
15. Move your hands up, slowly, to the tops of your shoulders. Let your arms cross over the center of your chest, without restricting your energy flow. Hold this position for around 3 minutes.
16. Relax your shoulders, and let that tension trickle down through the rest of your body as it releases. Feel where the energy goes, how it travels through your body, and the paths it takes.
17. Move your hands down to your sides, over each hip bone. Hold your hands there for around 3 minutes, and take time to notice the symmetry of your body.
18. Reflect on the balance that comes naturally with your form. As you inhale, feel the way your chest rises, and straightens your back with it. Concentrate on the connectedness of your body, and the energy that cycles through it.
19. Slowly bend over, or cross your legs, to reach the tops or soles of your feet. This is another highly concentrated area of energy on your body. Hold your hands here for 3 minutes, or longer, if you feel comfortable.

20. Imagine the palms of your hands lightly kissing the warmth of your feet. Visualize the work that you put your body through, the weight of you that your feet support, the labor your hands work for you.
21. Come back to center, and find a relaxing, neutral position. Hold for another 3 minutes here as you bring your attention back to your breathing.
22. When you're finished, take time to reflect on the exercise. How did you feel before it started? How do you feel now? Are there any positions that stood out to you during the session? Feel free to write these down, to create a record of the effect Reiki has on your spiritual growth.

Crystal Healing

The use of healing crystals has origins in Hinduism, Buddhism, and ancient spiritual medicine across the world (Rekstis, 2018). These stones are known for being excellent conduits for spiritual energy, each imbued with potent elements of the earth from which they were pulled. Each individual crystal has its own particular frequency of vibration, and these can have an effect when they resonate with someone's spiritual energy. This is how they can be used to aid in healing, and alter your energetic aura.

By resonating with the energetic frequencies of different crystals, you can open up your spiritual pathways to outside influence. This makes it easier for you to manipulate your energetic flow, and impact the health of your mind and body.

Crystals can offer a number of effects that soothe the mind and strengthen the relationship between your mental and spiritual energies. Some of these benefits include inner growth, emotional stability, reduced anxiety, and increased enthusiasm (Rekstis, 2018). Different crystals can be used to add a balancing frequency to your natural mental flow, influencing the ratio of positive to negative energy.

Similarly, these frequencies can travel through the relationship between your spirit and body. The physical benefits of crystal healing are numerous. For instance, you can use crystal healing to boost your immune system, soothe joint pain, relieve headaches, and help you sleep (Rekstis, 2018). These effects are more potent when the crystals are used as a conduit for spiritual energy from other holistic practices. By channeling your meditation, yogic alignment, or Reiki exercises through crystals, you can alter the resonating frequency of your healing energy.

People implement the use of healing crystals in many different ways. Some individuals feel comforted by simply holding the crystals during healing exercises, or keeping them in their healing environment, but it doesn't hurt to be a little creative.

One of the easiest, and most popular ways to benefit from the abundant healing power of crystals is through spiritual jewelry. Earrings, necklaces, bracelets, and piercings can all use crystals as an aesthetically pleasing way to channel spiritual energy. Crystals are naturally beautiful, and there is nothing wrong with wearing them for that purpose. Enjoying the way a crystal looks, or even the way you look while wearing it, adds its own mental and spiritual benefits to your life. Self-confidence is holistically healthy, and sometimes your appearance has an effect on that.

If you're religious, crystals can also make for great prayer beads or cross charms (Rekstis, 2018). Many people who integrate their spiritual practice with their faith find great benefit in using crystals as a conduit for their religious practices. This could aid in channeling prayer energy, increasing your connection to God, or pairing confession with cleansing techniques.

There is a diverse array of other ways you can add crystals to your life in subtle or aesthetically pleasing ways. Coasters, dishware, cosmetics, house decorations, and windchimes are just a few more examples of crystalware I own. If you happen to be a user of medical marijuana, they even make pipes out of healing crystals, to increase the spiritual potency of your herbal treatment (Rekstis, 2018).

Now, if you own healing crystals, you should make sure you are maintaining them to keep their quality from diminishing over time. Stones are pretty sturdy, so it's unlikely that they'll shatter, but they can still acquire some wear and tear. This comes from the fact that these crystals have such a strong ability to absorb the energy around them. With regular use, negative energy can cling to the crystal and remain in the stone after the session is over (Rekstis, 2018). Over time, this can build up, and reduce the crystal's effectiveness.

To prevent this, all you have to do is take care of your crystal with the same frequent attention you would give to expensive glassware, or your favorite tool. The first time you bring it home, and after every healing session, you should run your crystal under cool water to cleanse it of any lingering energy. Leaving them to dry out in natural sunlight or moonlight can help infuse positive energy back into the stone (Rekstis, 2018).

If you had a particularly intense experience during the session, or otherwise feel that it needs extra cleansing, you can add sea salt to the rinsing process. Sage smoke can also help cleanse anything, creating a powerful aura around your crystal through spiritual burning (Rekstis, 2018).

Ultimately, you should consider this maintenance an extended part of your healing session. These acts are not only important to the health of your crystal; they also reinforce self-discipline and mindful preservation of a healthy environment. This will bring you back to the values that are central to your practice of spiritual medicine.

I wanted to conclude this section with some of the crystals I've used in my personal practice and when healing others. These stones can be used to channel general healing energy, or for specific holistic benefits. You don't have to spend a lot of money on crystals in order for them to work. If you find simple versions of these stones that you like, and feel a connection with, go with those before you shell out on a larger, fancier version. Furthermore, if you can't find a particular crystal, you should be able to locate a different type of stone that offers similar healing benefits.

Don't limit yourself too much. Any crystal can be imbued with your healing energy and act as a conduit for your specific spiritual needs.

Sapphire	Promotes intuitive strength and wisdom; treats symptoms of depression, insomnia, and anxiety
Ruby	Attracts truthfulness and sincerity; cleanses toxins from the body
Moonstone	Strengthens the inner self and inspires growth; reduces stress and pessimistic thoughts
Bloodstone	Cleanses the blood and wards off negative environmental energies; improves circulation and strengthens the heart
Turquoise	Naturally strong healing energies, promotes emotional balance and stability; boosts the immune system and relieves skeletal aches
Citrine	Inspires joyfulness, optimism, and fearlessness
Amethyst	Purifies negative energies and promotes sincerity; Relieves symptoms of insomnia and stress

Jasper	Empowers the user, and naturally strengthens the spirit with its innate nurturing energy
Rose Quartz	Attracts love, increases libido, inspires passion and comfort
Clear Quartz	Reinforces balance, serves as a natural energy amplifier; Considered a "master healer" for its flexible nature
Obsidian	Natural protective energies, wards off negative energy and disruptive forces

Information outlined in this chart was sourced from Emily Rekstis in her article *Healing Crystals, 101*, written for Healthline (Rekstits, 2019)

Know Your Spirit

The best thing you can do for the health of your spiritual channels is to get to know it as if you were talking to another version of yourself in the mirror. This energy is unique to you, and made up of everything that influences your environment. If you spend time surrounded by negative influences, those energies will gradually become a part of you. You can't eliminate them without turning inward and finding the part of you that has changed.

This next, final chapter focuses on meditation. In some ways, I consider it an extension of this chapter, because it teaches you to harness these energetic channels that you've strengthened through the use of your spiritual practice. It would be a lie to say that meditation is an entirely spirit-based practice, though. Meditating is a fully holistic exercise that draws from what you've learned about the mind, body, and spirit, so I've included examples that combine those factors for you.

When you meditate for your health, make sure that you take time to understand that this is an act of opening. You are taking time to look into that mirror, examine what's inside, and really scrutinize yourself. You might not always like what you find at first, but over time, you'll get to know it better. Understanding the parts that work together to create your broader self will lead you to being a more functional person, and a stronger healer.

Chapter 6:

Meditation

My absolute favorite part of the day is my dedicated meditation session. I set out an hour after work for spiritual meditation during the week, and two hours after dinner on the weekend. Throughout the day, I get to look forward to a period of deep relaxation and insights about myself that stick with me until the next day. By setting a scheduled session at the same time each day, I've trained myself to expect that personal growth cycle throughout the week.

This enables me to experience spiritual healing during the session itself, and to form healthy habits outside of the exercise. In the unfortunate circumstance that I get busy and have to miss a session, I'm still engaging with self-discipline and introspection during that period. I don't have to force myself to make this happen; I'm simply so used to entering that state of mind in the evening that it naturally occurs, even when I'm not meditating.

Meditation is an extremely diverse practice that can take many different forms. Throughout your spiritual medicine experience, you will encounter certain meditations that work for you, and ones that don't. This is a normal part of exploring a new healing technique, and a testament to the broadness of the art.

This chapter is entirely dedicated to meditations I love, and instructions on how to perform them at home. If any of these appeal to you, try to incorporate them into a set schedule for yourself. This can be every day, every week, or even every month, depending on your personal life.

Be open and creative with these exercises, and always remember why you're doing them. Half the purpose of meditation is the intention you set at the beginning of the session. You should always enter a meditation exercise with a goal in mind, even if that goal is as simple as relaxation. If you feel the urge to add other components of holistic healing, or other "just for fun" twists, go ahead and do so. Your experience will be what you make of it, so nothing is against the rules.

Above all else, make sure that your meditation is centered on you. It should always be a reward for you to sit down and enter a session of spiritual healing. If you feel that you are overwhelmed with healing tasks, or that these exercises are too taxing for you, take a moment to evaluate what you have committed to. It can be easier than you think to overbook yourself, and sign up for more than your mind, body, and spirit are capable of. It never hurts to take things slow, or take a break, if you feel the need.

Preparing Yourself for Meditation

There are many things you should keep in mind as you start incorporating meditation into your regular routine.

Anyone can meditate, and you can gain benefits from the practice even in its lighter forms. Experts say that even 20 minutes of casual meditation every day can improve your health. In fact, the more hectic your life is, the more time you should set aside for meditative treatment (Bertone, 2020). The act of being mindful, and dedicating attention to your inner stability, is a fundamental form of self-care.

That being said, meditation isn't easy. Beginners should start with small sessions at first. If you've never meditated before, or find it challenging, you can begin with 5-10 minute exercises (Bertone, 2020). Even these bite-sized sessions can give you the vital fundamentals you need for productive spiritual healing.

For some people, occasional meditation can be used on an "as needed" basis. Bringing yourself in for sporadic self check-ins can help you monitor your holistic health and remind yourself to engage with self-care. That being said, if you're trying to live a fulfilling, holistic lifestyle, your meditation should be on a regular schedule.

I, personally, meditate every day at the same time. As long as you make an appointment for yourself, it can be as frequent as you feel is necessary. The important part is that you have a commitment to yourself, and you hold yourself to it. This is the first step to respecting your own health, and inviting yourself into the inner healing process.

You should also have a "safe space" that you use for any serious meditative exercise. This can be the same place that you engage with other spiritual medicine practices, but it should be dedicated to healing nonetheless. This should be a location that you feel ownership of, first and foremost. If you're in an unfamiliar area, where foreign energies overtake your own, you may find yourself distracted and restless during your experience. Having control over your physical space is a gateway to feeling control over your mind, body, and spirit. What you see and feel around you should reflect the way you want to feel inside.

To go a step further, you should also make this place feel special to you. Have fun with this part. Decorate your space with colors that make you feel powerful and energetic. Bring in spiritual aids like candles, incense, crystals, singing bowls, or music players. Anything that complements your practice has a place in this room. If possible, leave these objects in the room at all times, and their energies will infuse into the space.

Go ahead and do this with mundane things that you enjoy, as well. You should associate this area with positivity, even if it's just because of how it looks. If you like plants, keep your plants in there. If you love to paint, hang some of your art on the walls. Make this into somewhere that you're excited to go, and that you want to come back to for your next practice.

Synchronizing the Self

While there are many different styles of meditation, they all have one central focus in mind. By choosing to meditate, you are dedicating time and energy to bringing your mind, body, and spirit together. Unifying these elements of yourself is the key tenet of holistic medicine. Finding those connections between your thoughts, feelings, sensations, and spiritual energy allows you to synchronize them for a stronger core.

There are nine major categories of meditation that most exercises fall into. These types are designed, not to restrict the rules of any particular session, but to make it easier to compare techniques from one mediation to the other. Many specific exercises fit into more than one category, but their specific methodology and benefits can be explained using these terms. I like to think of them more as "focuses" than classifications.

These nine focuses are mindfulness meditation, concentrated meditation, divine meditation, mantra meditation, movement meditation, progressive meditation, transcendental meditation, visualization meditation, and loving-kindness meditation (Bertone, 2020). Each of these categories come with their type of intention that go along with it, and specific methodology that differs from case to case.

The focuses I like to use most in my practice are mindfulness, concentration, and visualization. These operate on the major principles that drive my healing exercises already, so they're easy to incorporate into my existing routines.

Each of these types of meditation bring your attention to your mind, body, and spirit in different ways. The process may be unique in each case, but the end goal is always the same. Finding that energetic connection within your holistic self is what gives meditation its power.

Mindfulness meditation is the form of meditation that you may be most familiar with. This is the type of meditative exercise that is most often portrayed in pop culture, and the majority of what people practice in America and Europe (Bertone, 2020). This form of meditation focuses on being aware of your unconscious thoughts, observing them while in an altered state, and learning from them. This is the most common type of meditation for many people because it centers around holistic fundamentals like introspection, concentration, and reflection.

The way that concentration meditation differs from this is not about the ultimate lesson, or the resulting synchronicity, but the way you get there. This type of meditation involves using an intense, focused activity, such as counting beads, braiding thread, or adult coloring, and using it as a vector for your meditative state. By pointing one of your senses on one particular repetitive task, you can aid the descent into an altered state of consciousness. This helps you get to that point where your unconscious thoughts are audible, and your energy is more suggestible to holistic methods.

For the remainder of this chapter, we'll go through some approachable meditative exercises that fit into these different categories. Some of these match a particular focus, while others are more of a mix. I prefer not to worry about the particular theory behind a meditation. Instead, I think more about the intent behind the act, and the meaning I imbue into the session.

This often leads me to creative, mixed meditations from multiple disciplines of spiritual medicine. I love to draw my latest "thing" into my meditations in order to deepen the session and heighten my experience with that new element. I chose to embrace that aspect for the examples I'm bringing to you. These exercises combine many of the techniques we've gone over already with the brilliant art of meditation.

As with everything else in this guide, find what your spiritual energy is most drawn to, and experiment with it. If half of one meditation works wonders for you, go ahead and slap it onto the other half of another exercise. There is no harm in working in pieces or lengthening one particularly effective.

Meditation for Relaxation

This exercise is a go-to meditation for reducing stress, anxiety, or general negative thoughts. Many people use meditation to heal these ailments, and bring peace to the restless mind. You can use almost any meditation for this purpose, but if calming down is your primary objective, this one will do the trick. These steps will run you through a mindful meditation designed to induce relaxation. It incorporates some aromatherapy oils to reduce anxiety, but feel free to use your preferred fragrance if you believe it will benefit your experience.

Steps:

1. Prepare your meditation space. This should be somewhere you feel comfortable, and will not be interrupted.

2. Light some incense or diffuse some essential oils into your space. For this meditation, I use lavender to help me detach from the stress of the day.
3. Find a comfortable place to sit or lie down. Take this moment for a few cycles of deep, natural breath. Find the scent in the room and notice how it makes you feel. What does it remind you of?
4. Next, set an intention for this exercise. If you came in with one in mind, go ahead and repeat that in your head, or whisper it out loud. If not, trust your instincts here, and find a goal that feels good to you in this moment. How do you want to feel at the end of this exercise? What would you like to discover?
5. Say the intention in your mind each time you inhale. Visualize the positive energy entering your body along with the breath.
6. Hold your breath for a few seconds after you inhale. Imbue that air with your intention, and let it absorb the energy of your desire.
7. When you exhale, release the thought completely. Visualize your breath flying out into the world, along with your words. Let them go.
8. Repeat this cycle, focusing on the ebb and flow of your intention. Concentrate on the air around you, the smell of it, and the way your body feels as you breathe.
9. Inhale, repeat your intention.

10. Hold, concentrating on how that intention makes you feel.
11. Exhale, releasing the thought. Return to the scent of the room, the feeling of air on your skin.
12. You can set a timer for 5-20 minutes for this exercise, or do it for as long as you feel comfortable.

Meditation for Visualization

As you may have noticed in the last exercises, visualization techniques can be used as features of many different types of meditation. Certain sessions, however, are dedicated to the act of visualization and affirmation. I use this next meditation exercise when I want to ruminate on a particular manifestation, or when I've been plagued by more negative thoughts than usual.

For the sake of this example, I am going to use one of the affirmations that I fall back to during times of stress: "I am stronger than I have ever been." This phrase helps me feel empowered, motivated, and connected to my body. It helps me acknowledge the growth I've already completed on my journey, and manifest a future where I continue to climb in success. If you like this affirmation, feel free to use it. I certainly didn't make it up, and it can help a lot of people. If you'd rather use an affirmation from the suggestions in Chapter 4, or one of your own, that's just as good. As long as the phrase means something to you, it can guide your visualization meditation in the right direction.

Steps:

1. Enter your meditative place, and find a comfortable seat. You should remove any distractions from this environment, and make sure you won't be interrupted.
2. Set your intention for the practice before you enter meditation. For visualization, this should be something specific about your inner desires. It can be a change you want to make in your life, better conditions for your environment, or anything else that would bring you positive energy in the future.
3. Once you have a clear goal, begin taking deep belly breaths. Let your eyes shut, and clear your mind of stray thoughts. If this is difficult for you, come back to your intention, and use it to find that blank slate.
4. Don't count your breaths, but take note of how they feel. Let your stomach rise and pull the air in deeper. When you exhale, feel the air blow between your lips, and enjoy the feeling of release.
5. When you're ready, picture what your future looks like, once this goal has been completed. For example, if you are trying to manifest a new career path, take time to imagine a day in the life of your dream job.

6. Start with the setting of your perfect future. Put yourself in your own personal office, decorate it piece by piece in your mind, take time to look out the window.
7. Let yourself linger in this picture for as long as you like. Make sure you keep the visual in your mind's eye, but continue to monitor your breaths.
8. If you find your mind wandering, or feel distracted, bring your focus back to your belly breaths for five deep cycles of air. Then, slowly add the details of your visualization back into the picture.
9. As the setting of your future takes shape, start to imagine more details about how it came to be. This could mean visualizing your drive to work every day, what you wear to the office, or how you tell your parents about the new position.
10. Acknowledge any emotions or sensations that come into being as you meditate. Don't reject these thoughts, even if they seem like distractions. Take time to understand what your mind is telling you, and then let it go back into the depths of your unconscious.
11. When you near the end of your session, bring your focus back to your belly breathing. Take five more cycles of breath before opening your eyes, and coming out of the meditation.

Meditation for Pain Relief

We all experience pain sometimes, and getting past it isn't always easy. Whether it's from a recovering injury, a chronic disease, or the natural aches that come with growing older, pain is hard to avoid in life. Medication, physical therapy, and special procedures can certainly go a long way in eliminating painful symptoms, but they are not always enough. Some conditions leave lasting discomfort even after treatment is complete, and people need a way to cope with that.

This is a concentrated meditation designed to relieve these common pains. It works by training you to focus attention on points of discomfort around your body. Then, through guided awareness, you can find the energy concentrated in those areas and redirect it.

I use amethyst crystal beads with this meditation for their natural soothing energy. Amethyst is great for relieving pain and reducing inflammation, which tends to be what causes me the most physical stress. The crystal serves as an open channel for me to release that negative energy into, and restore the natural flow of my healing power.

The beads serve as a concentration vector for me. While I meditate, I slowly count the beads, moving them one at a time between my fingers. This gives my body something to focus on separately from my mind and spirit. It helps me deepen the meditative state, and trains my mind to shut out the pain on command.

You don't have to use crystal beads for this meditation to help you. You can choose to use a regular crystal as a healing vector, or none at all. In the same way, you can use non-crystal beads as a concentration aid, or braided thread, or anything else that keeps your hands busy on a repetitive task.

Feel out what works best for you, and let it set the tone for your session. You'd be surprised what a random decision might tell you about yourself.

Steps:
1. Find a position where you feel most comfortable, depending on your source of pain. You should require no tension or force to keep yourself in this position for the entire session.
2. Shut your eyes, and take the crystal beads into your hands. Find an even rhythm in your breathing, and try to relax.
3. When you're ready to begin, start with a free exhale through your lips.
4. Inhale, and count to four. As you count, move one bead across the string for each count, in time with your breath.
5. Hold your breath, and count to seven. Again, move a bead with your fingers each time you count.
6. Exhale, and count to eight. Move each bead in time with the count, and concentrate on how they feel in your fingers. Note the temperature

of the crystal, the way it slides on the string, and the weight of it in your grasp.

7. Repeat this process a few times. Inhale 4, hold 7, exhale 8. For now, keep your mind focused on the task, the pattern, and the way it synchronizes with the rest of your body. How does the cycle of your breath affect your heart rate? How does the movement of your fingers line up with your state of mind?
8. Once you've gotten into the rhythm, gently direct your attention to the point of pain.
9. As you inhale for 4, focus on that location, how it feels, and experience it in full.
10. When you hold your breath for 7, visualize that part of your body. Picture the weight it holds in your day-to-day work, the movements it puts you through, the way it rests in your natural posture. Think of everything your body does for you.
11. Exhale for 8. Bring your focus back to your counting. As you release your breath, release all thoughts of pain, of your body, and of anything besides the beads.
12. Repeat this cycle as many times as you feel comfortable. If you find yourself dwelling on the pain too much, return your attention to the beads, and start again.
13. When you're ready to end your session, take a few cycles of breath without any counting, and gently stretch. Roll your shoulders, neck, and

ankles if it feels good. Take time to do things that make your body feel good, and end the meditation by focusing on those feelings.

Building Your Meditative Rhythm

As you find your footing, you'll find that certain aspects of spiritual medicine come naturally to you. This is because each and every one of these techniques is designed to work in conjunction with your innate power as a spiritual being. Your energetic channels have a specific wavelength at which they resonate with the world, simply as a result of existing within the interconnected web of the universe.

What many people do not understand about meditation is that it isn't a magic set of words and movements that erase your problems. It's a particular method crafted over thousands of years to guide the human consciousness closer to that spiritual power. These exercises are hard work, and require that intense dedication in order to meet their full potential.

When you come to your meditation session, you aren't just repeating it for the sake of memorization. It may feel like you're just trying to get things up to speed, or perfect a certain mantra, but I urge you to get out of that mindset if you're serious about spiritual medicine. The repetitive nature of meditative healing is about building up endurance in order to strengthen your energetic core.

Over time, you'll learn that you can feel the spirit's effect on your life, even when you aren't in the middle of a healing session. Just like professional runners get the itch to jog every morning, you'll find that desire to expand your spiritual practice.

Meditation, and spiritual medicine as a whole, is part of a larger cycle. If you remember one thing when continuing on your healing journey, let it be that. This cycle represents the flow of energy within yourself and out into the broader world, but it also represents the cycle of experience you will receive from dedicated spiritual healing.

The first time you experience a revelation about yourself, your spirit, or your purpose in life, it may seem like you've reached the end of your journey. If you continue your practice though, you'll find that new goals appear on the horizon. You can work towards bettering yourself over and over, and use that success to drive your healing going forward. This is the real cycle that you are participating in as you take control of your wellness.

Conclusion

The biggest misunderstanding that I run into with people outside of the spiritual medicine community, is that healing is supposed to work like a light switch. Skeptics like to point out people that are still experiencing pain, discomfort, anxiety, or any other common ailment after practicing traditional healing. They claim that these individuals are evidence that our methods don't work, or don't do any good for the patients who practice them. In reality, this perspective is only missing the point of healing as a process.

By now, you should have a good understanding of holistic health. The fact of the matter is that we are not sacks of meat with the sole purpose of eating food, reproducing, and sleeping. This would be a sad reality to live in. Human beings are intelligent, durable, energetic beings full of complexities. Our mind, body, and spirit each hold independent roles in the health of the whole. Without paying attention to the way these elements interact with each other, we ignore the full scope of the self.

Furthermore, this same principle applies to the relationship between the self and its environment. There is no doubt that the people, places, and possessions that you surround yourself with has a direct influence on your overall health. An unhealthy environment can lead to lifestyle choices like substance abuse, sluggishness, or overspending. Inevitably, these things lead to symptoms of mental illness, physical ailments, or a stunted spirit. The energy of your surroundings is the same energy you live, breathe, and sleep in. This has an effect on the way you feel.

Fortunately, these connections are things we have control over. Hopefully, through the examples in this guide, you've learned that your spiritual energy is malleable and potent. With the right practice, you'll find that the only limitation to your own personal growth is your dedication.

As you bring spiritual medicine into new parts of your life, you might find resistance along the way. The media presents traditional health care in a way that is completely misrepresentative of the fulfilling community that practices it.

If you encounter someone that holds these beliefs, don't let them add negative energy to your process. Instead, take time to explain what you gain from spiritual medicine, and invite them to join you for a healing session if you feel comfortable. Many people are afraid of the unknown, especially when it has to do with the most vulnerable parts of their lives.

Introspective thoughts, intense feelings, and even physical pain can be embarrassing for a lot of people. This is true for almost everyone. Spiritual medicine techniques excel at working with this problem, since it's centered around the idea of personal exploration. By learning to turn inward and acknowledge the power of your true self, you are actually strengthening yourself against these natural fears.

Those who are comfortable practicing holistic healing are more confident, self-assured, and motivated than skeptics who think of these practices as "silly." This is a toxic obsession that modern culture has with being rational, emotionless, and cold. Without the ability to embrace these hidden parts of ourselves, we starve them out, and cut ourselves off from our natural power.

The Old and the New

We are fortunate enough to live in a time that was built for us by millenia of ancestors. The oldest religions in the world show us the values humans have had since they were able to write them down. Even 5000 years ago, traditional Chinese healers used the same techniques that naturopaths use today, in order to bring spiritual unity into their medical practice (Callaghan, 2017). Personally, I find this extremely inspiring. The way humans wield their power in different ways, throughout history, has brought us so many unique ways to engage with the culture surrounding spiritual medicine.

The fact that these practices still exist today is incredible. This attests to the sturdy, reliable nature of holistic techniques. No matter how much society advances, the essential facts of our lives don't change all that much.

Instead, the environments around us shift drastically over time. In today's world, there are so many things to keep track of in order to maintain a healthy lifestyle.

Politics, finances, materialism, and relationships are just a few common sources of stress these days. Sometimes, they seem unavoidable. With the state of modern media, we are exposed to more negativity than we ever have been, as a population.

This can be a source of great imbalance in people's lives. A pessimist may linger on these facts, and worry over the state of the future. I refuse to see things that way.

We didn't have Facebook or Twitter 5000 years ago to remind us of all the problems that plagued humankind. This doesn't mean there weren't just as many of those problems. Civilizations have gone through wars, genocides, revolutions, and much, much more, but there has been one source of stability throughout this history. People have always sought out holistic healing, and developed their own traditional medicine, no matter what the world was going through.

Humans have an innate connection to their spiritual energy, and that connection brings us back to the same methods over and over. As an unspoken promise, people all over the world consistently develop cultures based around finding connections with this energy, and healing from within.

This is not changing any time soon. No matter how bleak the world looks on the news, I look to my community and see growth. In the 21st century, over one third of American medical schools, and over half world-wide, offer holistic health care courses. According to WHO, over 65% of people use holistic techniques as a primary source of health care. In a

United States survey, 74% of respondents indicated that they want a more natural approach to healthcare overall (Neddermeyer, 2009).

These are just a few statistics that show a rise in the acceptance of spiritual medicine. To me, this shows a positive trend in the energetic health of humankind as a whole. The energy that exists in each of us as individuals is a part of that larger spiritual network. When more people engage with their spiritual energy, that energetic flow is stronger for all of us. Our minds, bodies, and spirits are not only connected within the self, but in the broader universe itself.

I want to conclude this guide on this note by emphasizing this fact. The health of our world works on the same principle as the health of our self. When one part is ill, the whole suffers. As the population of spiritual healers increases, I believe that we will see an increase in global health. This will make for brighter personalities, more active communities, and a deeper sense of connection with one another.

As you embark on your healing journey, you will often feel the urge to look back. At times, you may reflect on your history, and feel ashamed of who you used to be. At others, you may even feel that you've worsened over time, and wish to go back to that older self. Take time to reject this linear understanding of your healing process. You should never compare yourself to yourself in this way. Debating which version of you is better or worse will only leave you feeling bad about who you are, one way or another.

Instead, think of your healing experience as a rich history. Just like our ancestors, 5000 years ago, your past self laid the groundwork for the state you find yourself in now. The growth you've experienced has not left that old life behind; it has built upon it. Without the pains, problems, and purpose that you held before, you would never be inspired to find your spirit to begin with. An unhealthy life is a starting point with a lot of potential. Even the most traumatic experiences are part of your path, in this way.

This is why I love to look to the future. The same things that inspire me about the fate of spiritual medicine, also inspire me about my personal spiritual process. I'm not done healing yet, and I don't think I ever will be. I've gotten better and worse at certain things over the years. The fact that I'm able to reflect, and evaluate those things shows that I've become a more conscious person overall. In the future, I'll learn even more about myself and my needs, by reinforcing my healing even more. I hope the same for you.

Let's conclude this guide with this intention in mind. Take a moment to reflect on what you've learned throughout this process, and what you hope for the future. Visualize the version of yourself that exists in steps to come. This self is happier, healthier, well-rounded, and energetic. Take a moment to reflect on what that looks like, and how it makes you feel.

Find affirmation in these thoughts, and let them resonate with you on your journey. This is about more than starts and endings, it's about you, yourself, and your spirit.

You are better than your past, and more than your future. You are the connection between the old and the new. You are the places in between.

What Next?

From here, you are in charge of where your healing takes you. The relationship you have with your spiritual energy is always going to change, and you're in the best position to identify what it needs. You might find that a particular practice highlighted in this book has made you want for more. Now that you've been introduced to your own healing energy, you can polish that relationship and discover what it's truly capable of.

Some people find fulfillment from healing in the home. Being in charge of your own practice can give you agency and creative control over the process. This is one of many advantages of holistic techniques, since they require little to no special equipment.

That being said, a great way to explore new aspects of spiritual medicine is by seeing a professional or joining a community of other healers. Reiki, acupressure, yoga, and meditation are all great techniques to take into a group setting. Making your practice a social experience can motivate you to show up on schedule, and provide a positive association from other people's energetic wavelengths.

Honestly, the best way to decide your next step is to meditate on the subject. If you feel indecisive, find an introspective exercise that you enjoy, and take time to think in peace. Your unconscious will guide you towards the experiences that have had the biggest impact on you.

For readers interested in the feminine side of spirituality, these ideas are explored from a holistic woman's perspective in our sister book Sacred Woman. If you haven't looked into it already, and you're looking for more literature to guide your healing process, give it a chance. Whether you're a spiritual woman or someone else who wants to explore their natural feminine energy, this book provides a look into the relationship between the female essence and traditional medicine.

References

AANMC. (2020, March 9). *10 Common Myths About Naturopathic Medicine.* AANMC. https://aanmc.org/featured-articles/10-common-myths-about-naturopathic-medicine/

Astrow, A., Puchalski, C., & Sumalsy, D. (2001). Religion, spirituality, and health care: social, ethical, and practical considerations. *The American Journal of Medicine, 110*(4), 283–287. https://doi.org/10.1016/s0002-9343(00)00708-7

Bernstein, G. (2019, July 27). *Practice Creative Visualization to Manifest the Life You Want.* Gabby Bernstein. https://gabbybernstein.com/get-miracle-train-practice-creative-visualization/

Bertone, H. (2020, September 17). *Which Type of Meditation Is Right for You?* Healthline. https://www.healthline.com/health/mental-health/types-of-meditation#getting-started

Brazier, Y. (2017, March 20). *Aromatherapy: Uses, benefits, oils, and risks.* Medical News Today. https://www.medicalnewstoday.com/articles/10884

Callaghan, R. (2017, January 6). *The History of 12 Ancient Medicines and Healers*. Selfcare.Global. https://selfcare.global/history-of-12-ancient-medicines-and-healers/

Cleveland Clinic. (2019, March 20). *Reiki Self-Treatment Procedure Details*. Cleveland Clinic. https://my.clevelandclinic.org/health/treatments/21080-reiki-self-treatment/procedure-details

Cronkleton, E. (2019, April 29). *Breathwork Basics, Uses, and Types*. Healthline. https://www.healthline.com/health/breathwork#exercises

Fletcher, J. (2019, March 13). *Hand pressure points: Chart and uses*. Medical News Today. https://www.medicalnewstoday.com/articles/324699#hand-pressure-points

Fox, M. (2016, March 22). *Fewer Americans Believe in God — Yet They Still Believe in Afterlife*. NBC News. https://www.nbcnews.com/better/wellness/fewer-americans-believe-god-yet-they-still-believe-afterlife-n542966

Gabriel, R. (2018, August 24). *The Chopra Center*. The Chopra Center. https://chopra.com/articles/yoga-sutras-101-everything-you-need-to-know

Gotter, A. (2017, March 23). *Box Breathing*. Healthline. https://www.healthline.com/health/box-breathing#exhale-again

Gotter, A. (2018, April 20). *4-7-8 Breathing: How It Works, How to Do It, and More*. Healthline. https://www.healthline.com/health/4-7-8-breathing#How-to-do-it

Healthwise. (2019, June 26). *Bodywork and Manual Therapy | Michigan Medicine*. Www.Uofmhealth.org. https://www.uofmhealth.org/health-library/aa104339spec#:~:text=The%20idea%20behind%20bodywork%20is

Hitti, M. (2011, March 2). *What Is Holistic Medicine?* WebMD; WebMD. https://www.webmd.com/balance/guide/what-is-holistic-medicine#1

Jewell, T. (2018, September 25). *Diaphragmatic Breathing and Its Benefits*. Healthline. https://www.healthline.com/health/diaphragmatic-breathing#steps-to-do

Kaiser, L. (2000). "Spirituality and the Physician Executive: Reconciling the Inner Self and the Business of Health Care. *The Physician Executive*, *26*(2).

Lindberg, S. (2020, August 24). *What Are Chakras? Meaning, Location, and How to Unblock Them*. Healthline. https://www.healthline.com/health/what-are-chakras#how-to-unblock-a-chakra

Mason, S. (2010). *Spiritual Healing: What is it? Does it work and does it have a place in modern healthcare?*

https://www.rcpsych.ac.uk/docs/default-source/members/sigs/spirituality-spsig/su-mason-spiritual-healing-in-modern-healthcare-x.pdf?sfvrsn=4fc21449_2

MHA. (2012). *The State of Mental Health in America | Mental Health America.* Mhanational.org. https://www.mhanational.org/issues/state-mental-health-america

Mohr, W. (2006). Spiritual Issues in Psychiatric Care. *Perspectives in Psychiatric Care, 42*(3), 174–183.

Neddermeyer, D. (2009, January 16). *Holistic Health Care Facts and Statistics.* Disabled World. https://www.disabled-world.com/medical/alternative/holistic/care-statistics.php

Newman, T. (2017, September 6). *Reiki: What is it and are there benefits?* Medical News Today. https://www.medicalnewstoday.com/articles/308772#what-happens-in-a-reiki-session

Pietrangelo, A. (2020, March 29). *The Effects of Stress on Your Body.* Healthline. https://www.healthline.com/health/stress/effects-on-body#7

Rakicevic, M. (2020, January 14). *31 Yoga Statistics: The Modern World Embraces Yoga.* DisturbMeNot! https://disturbmenot.co/yoga-statistics/#:~:text=300%20million%20people%20do%20yoga

Rekstis, E. (2018, June 21). *Healing Crystals 101.* Healthline; Healthline Media. https://www.healthline.com/health/mental-health/guide-to-healing-crystals

Rodriguez, E. (2016, August 30). *Acupressure Points: How Do They Work in Massage?* Www.Amcollege.Edu. https://www.amcollege.edu/blog/acupressure-points-how-they-work-massage

Rose, A. (2019, May 16). *7 steps to Energetic Alignment.* Thriveglobal.com. https://thriveglobal.com/stories/7-steps-to-energetic-alignment/

Scott, E. (2020, October). *4 Ways to Surround Yourself with Positive Energy.* Verywell Mind. https://www.verywellmind.com/reduce-stress-positive-energy-3144815

Silver, V. (2011, October 7). *What Is Holistic Spirituality?* Yoga Flavored Life. https://www.yogaflavoredlife.com/what-is-holistic-spirituality/

Tanner Clinic. (2020, January 29). *How Mental Health Affects Physical Health.* Tanner Clinic. https://tannerclinic.com/news/how-your-mental-health-affects-your-physical-well-being/

Manufactured by Amazon.ca
Bolton, ON